About Island Press

Since 1984, the nonprofit Island Press has been stimulating, shaping, and communicating the ideas that are essential for solving environmental problems worldwide. With more than 800 titles in print and some 40 new releases each year, we are the nation's leading publisher on environmental issues. We identify innovative thinkers and emerging trends in the environmental field. We work with world-renowned experts and authors to develop cross-disciplinary solutions to environmental challenges.

Island Press designs and implements coordinated book publication campaigns in order to communicate our critical messages in print, in person, and online using the latest technologies, programs, and the media. Our goal: to reach targeted audiences—scientists, policymakers, environmental advocates, the media, and concerned citizens—who can and will take action to protect the plants and animals that enrich our world, the ecosystems we need to survive, the water we drink, and the air we breathe.

Island Press gratefully acknowledges the support of its work by the Agua Fund, Inc., The Margaret A. Cargill Foundation, Betsy and Jesse Fink Foundation, The William and Flora Hewlett Foundation, The Kresge Foundation, The Forrest and Frances Lattner Foundation, The Andrew W. Mellon Foundation, The Curtis and Edith Munson Foundation, The Overbrook Foundation, The David and Lucile Packard Foundation, The Summit Foundation, Trust for Architectural Easements, The Winslow Foundation, and other generous donors.

The opinions expressed in this book are those of the author(s) and do not necessarily reflect the views of our donors.

Measuring Urban Design

Metropolitan Planning + Design
Series editors: Arthur C. Nelson and Reid Ewing

A collaboration between Island Press and the University of Utah's Department of City & Metropolitan Planning, this series provides a set of tools for students and professionals working to make our cities and metropolitan areas more sustainable, livable, prosperous, resilient, and equitable. As the world's population grows to nine billion by mid-century, the population of the US will rise to one-half billion. Along the way, the physical landscape will be transformed. Indeed, two-thirds of the built environment in the US at mid-century will be constructed between now and then, presenting a monumental opportunity to reshape the places we live. The *Metropolitan Planning + Design* series presents an integrated approach to addressing this challenge, involving the fields of planning, architecture, landscape architecture, urban design, public policy, environmental studies, geography, and civil and environmental engineering. The series draws from the expertise of some of the world's leading scholars in the field of Metropolitan Planning + Design.

Please see Islandpress.org/Utah/ for more information.

Other books in the series:
The TDR Handbook, Arthur C. Nelson, Rick Pruetz, and
    Doug Woodruff (2011)
Stewardship of the Built Environment, Robert Young (2012)
Governance and Equity, Marc Brenman and Thomas W.
    Sanchez (2012)
Good Urbanism: Six Steps to Creating Prosperous Places,
    Nan Ellin (2012)

Measuring
Urban Design

Metrics for Livable Places

Reid Ewing & Otto Clemente

with

Kathryn M. Neckerman
Marnie Purciel-Hill
James W. Quinn
Andrew Rundle

Washington | Covelo | London

ISLAND PRESS is a trademark of The Center for Resource Economics.

Library of Congress Cataloging-in-Publication Data

Ewing, Reid H.

    Measuring urban design : metrics for livable places / Reid Ewing and Otto Clemente with Kathryn M. Neckerman, Marnie Purciel-Hill, James W. Quinn, Andrew Rundle.

          pages cm

Summary: "What makes strolling down a particular street enjoyable? The authors of Measuring Urban Design argue it's not an idle question. Inviting streets are the centerpiece of thriving, sustainable communities, but it can be difficult to pinpoint the precise design elements that make an area appealing. This accessible guide removes the mystery, providing clear methods to assess urban design. The book provides operational definitions and measurement protocols of five intangible qualities of urban design, specifically: imageability, visual enclosure, human scale, transparency, and complexity. The result is a reliable field survey instrument grounded in constructs from architecture, urban design, and planning. Readers will also find illustrated, step-by-step instructions to use the instrument and a scoring sheet for easy calculation of urban design quality scores"--Provided by publisher.

    Includes bibliographical references and index.
    ISBN-13: 978-1-61091-193-1 (hardback)
    ISBN-10: 1-61091-193-8 (cloth)
    ISBN-13: 978-1-61091-194-8 (paper)

1. City planning--Social aspects. 2. Architecture--Human factors. 3. City planning--Methodology. I. Clemente, Otto. II. Title.

    NA9053.H76E95 2013
    711'.4—dc23

Printed on recycled, acid-free paper

Manufactured in the United States of America

10 9 8 7 6 5 4 3 2 1

Key Words: Columbia's Built Environment and Health (BEH) group, complexity, human scale, D variables, imageability, Maryland Inventory of Urban Design Qualities (MIUDQ) protocol, legibility, linkage, perceptual qualities, Robert Wood Johnson Active Living Research (ALR), sidewalk connection, tidiness, transparency, visual enclosure, visual preference survey

Contents

Acknowledgments

This book is the result of an interdisciplinary, inter-university collaboration. Susan Handy, a professor of environmental policy at UC Davis, and Ross Brownson, an epidemiologist at Washington University in St. Louis, were full partners in the original study funded under the Robert Wood Johnson's Active Living Research Program, Round 1, Identifying and Measuring Environmental Determinants of Physical Activity (grant # 50337). Susan is a leading researcher on the relationship between land use and travel. She has done seminal research on the factors that affect walking. Ross is regarded as one of the leaders in the field of evidence-based public health. He co-directs the Prevention Research Center in St. Louis—a major, CDC funded center jointly led by Washington University and Saint Louis University. Susan and I co-authored the article upon which Chapter 1 is based: "Measuring the Unmeasurable: Measuring the Unmeasurable: Urban Design Qualities Related to Walkability." Ross and Susan participated in all phases of the ALR project as described in Chapters 2 and 3.

Additional collaborators include Kathy Neckerman and Andrew Rundle's team at Columbia University, whose research is described in Chapter 4. They too were funded under the Active Living Research Program of the Robert Wood Johnson Foundation (grant #58089). Kathy is a sociologist at the Columbia Population Research Center and Andrew is an epidemiologist at Columbia's Mailman School of Public Health. They co-direct the Built Environment and Health (BEH) research group at Columbia and have written extensively about disparities in neighborhood conditions and their implications for health and wellbeing.

The validation exercise in Chapter 5 involved several students and staff at the University of Utah: Mark Connors, Amir Hajrasouliha, Shima Hamidi, and J.P. Goates. J.P. generated GIS measures for buffers around the 588 sampled street segments in New York City. Mark, Amir, and Shima counted pedestrians in street-level imagery and comparing these counts to the manual counts.

The team at Island Press who took this book to publication includes senior editor Heather Boyer, associate editor Courtney Lix, and senior production editor Sharis Simonian. Their professionalism is evident in the final product. To all of the above, we say thanks.

Reid Ewing and Otto Clemente

CHAPTER ONE

Introduction[1]

In terms of the public realm, no element is more important than streets. This is where active travel to work, shop, eat out, and engage in other daily activities takes place, and where walking for exercise mostly occurs. Parks, plazas, trails, and other public places also have an important role in physical activity, but given the critical role and ubiquity of streets, this book focuses on the qualities that make one street more inviting and walkable than another. Think of your last trip to a great European city and what, other than the historic structures and the food, was memorable. You walked its streets for hours and did not tire. It is the magic of a great street environment.

Until recently, the measures used to characterize the built environment have been mostly gross qualities such as neighborhood density and street connectivity (see reviews by Ewing and Cervero 2010; Handy 2005; and Ewing 2005). The urban design literature points to subtler qualities that may influence choices about active travel and active leisure time. Referred to as perceptual qualities of the urban environment, or urban design qualities, such qualities are presumed to intervene between physical features and behavior, encouraging people to walk (see figure 1.1). Testing this presumption requires reliable methods of measuring urban design qualities, allowing comparison of these qualities to walking behavior.

Many tools for measuring the quality of the walking environment have emerged in the past few years. Generically called walking audit instruments, these are now used across the United States by researchers, local governments, and community groups. Robert Wood Johnson's Active Living Research

---

[1] This chapter is adapted with permission from R. Ewing and S. Handy, "Measuring the Unmeasurable: Urban Design Qualities Related to Walkability," *Journal of Urban Design* 14, no. 1 (2009): 65–84. The research reported in chapters 1–3 and 6 was supported by the Robert Wood Johnson Foundation Active Living Research under grant #50337.

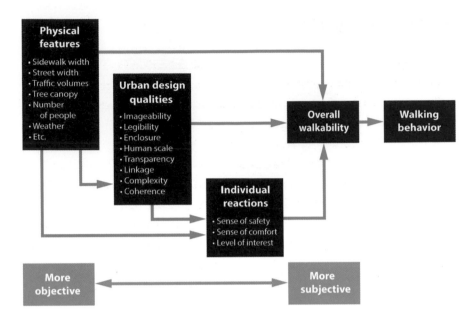

Figure 1.1.

(ALR) website alone hosts sixteen walking audit instruments. They involve the measurement of such physical features as building height, block length, and street and sidewalk width.

Urban design qualities are more than the individual physical features that they comprise, as they have a cumulative effect that is greater than the sum of the parts. Physical features individually may not tell us much about the experience of walking down a particular street. Specifically, they do not capture people's overall perceptions of the street environment, perceptions that may have complex or subtle relationships to physical features.

Perceptual qualities are also different from such qualities as sense of comfort, sense of safety, and level of interest, which reflect how an individual reacts to a place—how a person assesses the conditions there, given his or her own attitudes and preferences. Perceptions are just that—perceptions. They may elicit different reactions in different people. They can be assessed objectively by outside observers; individual reactions cannot.

Our challenge in creating a tool to measure urban design qualities was to move from highly subjective definitions to operational definitions that capture the essence of each quality and can be measured reliably across raters, including those without training in urban design.

Why You Should Read This Book

Measuring Urban Design provides operational definitions and measurement protocols for five intangible qualities of urban design: imageability, visual enclosure, human scale, transparency, and complexity. To help disseminate these measures, this book also provides a field survey instrument that has been tested and refined for use by lay observers.

This instrument has several strengths. First, it is grounded conceptually in constructs from architecture, urban design, and planning. Second, it has been carefully tested and validated. Third, it comes with detailed instructions for assessing the five urban design qualities. For these reasons, the instrument offers researchers a "gold standard" for the systematic measurement of urban design. A test in New York City showed that the instrument can be implemented in large-scale studies relating the built environment to social, psychological, and health outcomes.

Initial Screening of Qualities

Key perceptual qualities of the urban environment were identified based on a review of the classic urban design literature. Without much empirical evidence, these qualities are presumed to influence people's decisions to walk rather than drive to a destination, stroll in their leisure time, or just hang out and socialize on a street. Perceptual qualities figure prominently in such classics as those listed in box 1.1.

The research team also reviewed the visual preference and assessment literatures, which attempt to measure how individuals perceive their environments and to better understand what individuals value in their environments. Partial listing of this voluminous empirical literature is provided in Ewing (2000) and updated in Ewing et al. (2005). These literature reviews go beyond the boundaries of urban design to the fields of architecture, landscape architecture, park planning, and environmental psychology, as perceptual qualities of the environment figure prominently in these fields as well.

Our review yielded a list of fifty-one perceptual qualities of the urban environment (box 1.2). Of these fifty-one qualities, eight were selected for further

Box 1.1.

Classic Works in Urban Design That Address Perceptual Qualities

City Planning according to Artistic Principles, Camillo Sitte, 1889 (complete English translation 1986)

The Image of the City, Kevin Lynch, 1960

The Concise Townscape, Gordon Cullen, 1961

The Death and Life of Great American Cities, Jane Jacobs, 1961

A Pattern Language: Towns, Buildings, Construction, Christopher Alexander, Sara Ishikawa, and Murray Silverstein, 1977

Fundamentals of Urban Design, Richard Hedman, 1984

Finding Lost Space: Theories of Urban Design, Roger Trancik, 1986

Life between Buildings: Using Public Space, Jan Gehl, 1987

City: Rediscovering the Center, William Whyte, 1988

Town Planning in Practice, Raymond Unwin, 1909

History and Precedent in Environmental Design, Amos Rapoport, 1990

Great Streets, Allan Jacobs, 1993

Trees in Urban Design, Henry Arnold, 1993

Box 1.2.

Fifty-One Perceptual Qualities of the Built Environment

adaptability	singularity	naturalness	identifiability	deflection
distinctiveness	clarity	texture	ornateness	interest
intricacy	enclosure	compatibility	upkeep	regularity
richness	meaning	formality	continuity	vividness
ambiguity	spaciousness	novelty	imageability	depth
diversity	coherence	transparency	prospect	intimacy
legibility	expectancy	complementarity	variety	rhythm
sensuousness	mystery	human scale	contrast	
centrality	territoriality	openness	intelligibility	
dominance	comfort	unity	refuge	
linkage	focality	complexity	visibility	

study based on the importance assigned to them in the literature: imageability, enclosure, human scale, transparency, complexity, coherence, legibility, and linkage. Of the eight, the first five were successfully measured in a manner that passed tests of validity and reliability.

Imageability

Imageability is the quality of a place that makes it distinct, recognizable, and memorable. A place has high imageability when specific physical elements and their arrangement capture attention, evoke feelings, and create a lasting impression. It is probably not one element by itself that makes a street imageable but rather the combination of many.

According to Kevin Lynch (1960), a highly imageable city is well formed, contains distinct parts, and is instantly recognizable to anyone who has visited or lived there. It plays to the innate human ability to see and remember patterns. It is a city whose elements are easily identifiable and grouped into an overall pattern.

Landmarks are a component of imageability. The term *landmark* does not necessarily denote a grandiose civic structure or even a large object. In the words of Lynch, it can be "a doorknob or a dome." What is essential is its singularity and location, in relationship to its context and the city at large. Landmarks are a principle of urban design because they act as visual termination points, orientation points, and points of contrast in an urban setting. Tunnard and Pushkarev (1963, p. 140) attribute even greater importance to landmarks, saying, "A landmark lifts a considerable area around itself out of anonymity, giving it identity and visual structure."

Figures 1.2a, b, c. Video clips shot at Fisherman's Wharf, San Francisco, CA, rating high in Imageability.

Imageability is related to "sense of place." Gorden Cullen (1961, p. 152) asserts that a characteristic visual theme will contribute to a cohesive sense of place and will inspire people to enter and rest in the space. Jan Gehl (1987, p. 183) explains this phenomena using the example of famous Italian city squares, where "life in the space, the climate, and the architectural quality support and complement each other to create an unforgettable total impression." When all factors manage to work together to such pleasing ends, a feeling of physical and psychological well-being results: the feeling that a space is a thoroughly pleasant place in which to be.

Imageability is influenced by many other urban design qualities—enclosure, human scale, transparency, complexity, coherence, legibility, and linkage—and is in some sense the net effect of these qualities. Places that rate high on these qualities are likely to rate high on imageability as well—the neighborhoods of Paris or San Francisco, for example. However, places that rate low on these qualities may also evoke strong images, though ones that people may prefer to forget. Urban designers focus on the strength of positive images in discussing imageability and sense of place.

A panel of experts we assembled most often mentioned vernacular architecture as a contributor to imageability (Ewing and Handy 2009). Other influences mentioned were landmarks, striking views, unusual topography, and marquee signage. Beyond Kevin Lynch's (1960) detailed qualitative characterizations, and two quantitative studies of building recall, we could find no attempts to operationalize imageability in either visual assessment studies or design guidelines.

Enclosure

Enclosure refers to the degree to which streets and other public spaces are visually defined by buildings, walls, trees, and other vertical elements. Spaces where the height of vertical elements is proportionally related to the width of the space between them have a room-like quality.

Outdoor spaces are defined and shaped by vertical elements, which interrupt viewers' lines of sight. A sense of enclosure results when lines of sight are so decisively blocked as to make outdoor spaces seem room-like. Cullen (1961, p. 29) states: "Enclosure, or the outdoor room, is, perhaps, the most powerful, the most obvious, of all the devices to instill a sense of position, of identity with the surroundings....It embodies the idea of hereness." Alexander, Ishikawa, and Silverstein (1977, p. 106) say that "an outdoor space is positive when it has a distinct and definite shape, as definite as the shape of a room, and when its shape is as important as the shapes of the buildings which surround it." Likewise, Jacobs and Appleyard (1987, p. 118) speak of the need for buildings to "define or even enclose space—rather than sit in space." Richard Hedman (1984) refers to certain arrangements of buildings as creating intensely three-dimensional spaces.

In an urban setting, enclosure is formed by lining the street or plaza with unbroken building fronts of roughly equal height. The buildings become the "walls" of the outdoor room, the street and sidewalks become the "floor," and if the buildings are roughly equal height, the sky projects as an invisible ceiling. Buildings lined up that way are often referred to as street walls. Alexander et al. (1977, pp. 489–91) state that the total width of the street, building to building, should not exceed the building heights in order to maintain a comfortable feeling of enclosure. Allan Jacobs (1993) is more liberal in this regard, suggesting that the proportion of building heights to street width should be at least 1:2. Other designers have recommended proportions as high as 3:2 and as low as 1:6 for a sense of enclosure.

At low suburban densities, building masses become less important in defining space, and street trees assume the dominant role. Rows of trees on both sides of a street can humanize the height-to-width ratio. Henry Arnold (1993) explains that trees define space both horizontally and vertically. Horizontally, they do so by visually enclosing or completing an

Figures 1.3a, b, c. Video clips shot in Charlotte, NC, rating high in Enclosure.

area of open space. Vertically, they define space by creating an airy ceiling of branches and leaves. Unlike the solid enclosure of buildings, tree lines depend on visual suggestion and illusion. Street space will seem enclosed only if trees are closely spaced. Properly scaled, walls and fences can also provide spatial definition in urban and suburban settings. Kevin Lynch (1962) recommended walls and fences that are either low or over six feet tall.

Visual termination points may also contribute to a sense of enclosure. Andres Duany and other new urbanists advocate closing vistas at street ends with prominent buildings, monuments, fountains, or other architectural elements as a way of achieving enclosure in all directions (Duany and Plater-Zyberk 1992). When a street is not strongly defined by buildings, focal points at its ends can maintain the visual linearity of the arrangement. Similarly, the layout of the street network can influence the sense of enclosure. A rectilinear grid with continuous streets creates long sight lines that may undermine the sense of enclosure created by the buildings and trees that line the street. Irregular grids may create visual termination points that help to enclose a space; cul-de-sacs, for example, tend to create more sense of enclosure than through streets.

Enclosure is eroded by breaks in the continuity of the street wall, that is, breaks in the vertical elements, such as buildings or tree rows, that line the street. Breaks in continuity that are occupied by inactive uses create dead spaces that further erode enclosure; vacant lots, parking lots, driveways, and other uses that do not generate human activity and presence are all considered dead spaces. Large building setbacks are another source of dead space. Alexander et al. (1997, p. 593) say that "building setbacks from the street, originally invented to protect the public welfare by giving every building light and air, have actually helped greatly to destroy the street as social space."

Our expert panel suggested that on-street parking, planted medians, and even traffic itself contribute to visual enclosure. They opined that the required building height to enclose street space varies with context, specifically, between a big city and a small town.

The visual assessment literature suggests that enclosure is an important factor in human responses to environments, and that solid surfaces are the important variable in impressions of enclosure. Using photographs of Paris, Stamps and Smith (2002) found that the perception of enclosure is positively related to the proportion of a scene covered by walls, and negatively related to the proportion of a scene consisting of ground, the depth of view, and the number of sides open at the front. These results were confirmed in later visual simulations (Stamps 2005).

Enclosure is defined both qualitatively and quantitatively in many urban design guidelines and several land development codes. The qualitative definitions sometimes capture the multifaceted nature of the concept, for example, in Denver, Colorado's design manual: "Building facades should closely align and create a continuous facade, punctuated by store entrances and windows. This produces a comfortable sense of enclosure for the pedestrian and a continuous storefront that attracts and encourages the pedestrian to continue along the street" (City of Denver 1993).

Human Scale

Human scale refers to a size, texture, and articulation of physical elements that match the size and proportions of humans and, equally important, correspond to the speed at which humans walk. Building details, pavement texture, street trees, and street furniture are all physical elements contributing to human scale.

The urban design glossary for the City of Seattle (2004) defines human scale as "the quality of a building that includes structural or architectural components of size and proportions that relate to the human form and/or that exhibits through its structural or architectural components the human functions contained within" (par. 57). Moderate-sized buildings, narrow streets, and small spaces create an intimate environment, and the opposite for tall buildings, wide streets, and large spaces.

Alexander et al. (1977) state that any buildings over four stories tall are out of human scale. Lennard and Lennard (1987) set the limit at six stories. Hans Blumenfeld (1953) sets it at three stories. In taller buildings, Roger Trancik (1986) says that lower floors should spread out and upper floors step back before they ascend, giving human-scale definition to streets and plazas. Richard Hedman (1984) emphasizes the importance of articulated architecture and belt courses and cornices on large buildings to help define street space and scale.

Several authors suggest that the width of buildings, not just the height, defines human scale. For human scale, building widths should not be out of proportion with building heights, as are so many buildings in the suburbs.

Human scale can also be defined by human speed. Jane Holtz Kay (1997) argues that today, far too many things are built to accommodate the bulk

Figures 1.4a, b, c. Video clips shot in Alexandria, VA, rating high in Human Scale.

and rapid speed of the automobile; we are "designing for 60 mph." When approached by foot, these things overwhelm the senses, creating disorientation. For example, large signs with large lettering are designed to be read by high-speed motorists. For pedestrians, small signs with small lettering are much more comfortable.

According to Alexander et al. (1977), a person's face is just recognizable at seventy feet, a loud voice can just be heard at seventy feet, and a person's face is recognizable in portrait-like detail up to about forty-eight feet. These lengths set the limits of human scale for social interaction.

Street trees can moderate the scale of tall buildings and wide streets. According to Henry Arnold (1993), where tall buildings or wide streets would intimidate pedestrians, a canopy of leaves and branches allows for a simultaneous experience of the smaller space within the larger volume. He posits that where streets are over forty feet wide, additional rows of trees are needed to achieve human scale. Hedman (1984) recommends the use of other small-scale elements, such as clock towers, to moderate the scale of buildings and streets.

In addition to the above elements, our expert panel related human scale to the intricacy of paving patterns, amount of street furniture, depth of setbacks on tall buildings, presence of parked cars, ornamentation of buildings, and spacing of windows and doors. Interestingly, high-rise Rockefeller Center and Times Square were both perceived as human scaled due to compensating design elements at street level.

Land development ordinances and urban design guidelines occasionally make reference to human scale as a desirable quality. The guidelines of Davis, California, define human scale in qualitative terms: "The size or proportion of a building element or space relative to the structural or functional dimensions of the human body. Used generally to refer to building elements that are smaller in scale, more proportional to the human body, rather than monumental (or larger scale)" (City of Davis 2007).

A few ordinances get more specific, for example, Placer County, California's:

> The relationship of a building, or portions of a building, to a human being is called its relationship to "human scale." The spectrum of relationships to human scale ranges from intimate to monumental. Intimate usually refers to small spaces or detail which is very much in keeping with the human scale, usually areas around eight to ten feet in size. These spaces feel intimate because of the relationship of a human being to the space. . . . The components of a building with an intimate scale are often small and include details which break those components into smaller units. At the other end of the spectrum, monumental scale is used to present a feeling of grandeur, security, timelessness, or spiritual well being. Building types which commonly use the monumental scale to express these feelings are banks, churches, and civic buildings. The components of this scale also reflect this grandness, with oversized double door entries, 18-foot glass storefronts, or two-story columns. (Placer County 2003)

To our knowledge, there has been only one previous attempt to operationalize human scale via a visual assessment survey, and this strictly with respect of architectural massing (Stamps 1998b). The most important determinant was the cross-sectional area of buildings, second was the amount of fenestration, and third was the amount of facade articulation and partitioning.

Transparency

Transparency refers to the degree to which people can see or perceive what lies beyond the edge of a street or other public space and, more specifically, the degree to which people can see or perceive human activity beyond the edge of a street or other public space. Physical elements that influence transparency

Figures 1.5a, b, c. Video clips shot in Washington, DC, rating high in Transparency.

include walls, windows, doors, fences, landscaping, and openings into midblock spaces.

Taken literally, transparency is a material condition that is pervious to light or air, an inherent quality of substance as in a glass wall. A classic example of transparency is a shopping street with display windows that invite passersby to look in and then come in to shop. Blank walls and reflective glass buildings are classic examples of design elements that destroy transparency.

But transparency can be subtler than this. What lies behind the street edge need only be imagined, not actually seen. Jacobs (1993) says that streets with many entryways contribute to the perception of human activity beyond the street, while those with blank walls and garages suggest that people are far away. Even blank walls may exhibit some transparency if overhung by trees or bushes, providing signs of habitation.

Arnold (1993) tells us that trees with high canopies create "partially transparent tents," affording awareness of the space beyond while still conferring a sense of enclosure. By contrast, small trees in most urban settings work against transparency (Arnold 1993).

Transparency is most critical at the street level, because this is where the greatest interaction occurs between indoors and outdoors. The ultimate in transparency is when internal activities are "externalized," or brought out to the sidewalk (Llewelyn–Davies 2000). Outdoor dining and outdoor merchandising are examples.

Our expert panel suggested that courtyards, signs, and buildings that convey specific uses (schools and churches) add to transparency. Reflective glass, arcades, and large building setbacks were thought to detract from transparency. Interior lighting, shadows, and reflections were also thought to have a role in the perception of transparency.

Transparency is the urban design quality most frequently defined in urban design guidelines and land development codes. Some definitions of transparency are strictly qualitative. Others are quantitative. The concept is operationalized almost always in limited terms of windows as a percentage of ground floor facade. San Jose's operational definition is typical:

> Transparency: A street level development standard that defines a requirement for clear or lightly tinted glass in terms of a percentage of the façade area between an area falling within 2 feet and 20 feet above the adjacent sidewalk or walkway. (City of San Jose 2004)

Complexity

Complexity refers to the visual richness of a place. The complexity of a place depends on the variety of the physical environment, specifically, the numbers and kinds of buildings, architectural diversity and ornamentation, landscape elements, street furniture, signage, and human activity.

Amos Rapoport (1990) explains the fundamental properties of complexity. Complexity is related to the number of noticeable differences to which a viewer is exposed per unit time. Human beings are most comfortable receiving information at perceivable rates. Too little information produces sensory deprivation; too much creates sensory overload. Rapoport contrasts the complexity requirements of pedestrians and motorists. Slow-moving pedestrians require a high level of complexity to hold their interest. Fast-moving motorists will find the same environment chaotic. The commercial strip is too complex and chaotic at driving speeds yet, due to scale, yields few noticeable differences at pedestrian speeds.

The environment can provide low levels of usable information in three ways: elements may be too few or too similar; elements, though numerous and varied, may be too predictable for surprise or novelty; or elements, though numerous and varied, may be too unordered for comprehension. Pedestrians are apt to prefer streets high in complexity, since they provide interesting things to look at: building details, signs, people, surfaces,

Figures 1.6a, b, c. Video clips shot in New York, NY, rating high in Complexity.

changing light patterns and movement, signs of habitation. As Jan Gehl (1987, p. 143) notes in his classic book *Life between Buildings*, an interesting walking network will have the "psychological effect of making the walking distance seem shorter" by virtue that the trip is "divided naturally, into manageable stages."

Complexity results from varying building shapes, sizes, materials, colors, architecture, and ornamentation. According to Jacobs and Appleyard (1987), narrow buildings in varying arrangements add to complexity, while wide buildings subtract. Allan Jacobs (1993) refers to the need for many different surfaces over which light is constantly moving in order to keep eyes engaged. Tony Nelessen (1994, p. 224) asserts that "variations on basic patterns must be encouraged in order to prevent a dull sameness. If a particular building or up to three buildings are merely repeated, the result will be boring and mass produced." Variation can be incorporated into the building orientation plan or building setback line, allowing for varied building frontage instead of monotonous, straight building frontage. Numerous doors and windows produce complexity as well as transparency.

Complexity is one perceptual quality that has been measured extensively in visual assessment studies. It has been related to changes in texture, width, height, and setback of buildings (Elshestaway 1997). It has also been related to building shapes, articulation, and ornamentation (Stamps 1998a, 1999; Heath, Smith, and Lim 2000).

Other elements of the built environment also contribute to complexity. According to Henry Arnold (1993), one function of trees is to restore the rich textural detail missing from modern architecture. Light filtered through trees gives life to space. Manipulation of light and shade transforms stone, asphalt, and concrete into tapestries of sunlight and shadow. Allan Jacobs (1993) similarly gives values to the constant movement of branches and leaves and to the ever-changing light that plays on, through, and around them. Street furniture also contributes to the complexity of street scenes. Jacobs (1993) states that pedestrian-scaled streetlights, fountains, carefully thought out benches, special paving, even public art, combine to make regal, special places.

Signage is a major source of complexity in urban and suburban areas. If well done, signs can add visual interest, make public spaces more inviting, and help create a sense of place. Cullen (1961, p. 151) calls advertisement signs "the most characteristic, and, potentially, the most valuable, contribution of the twentieth century to urban scenery." When these signs are lit up at night, the result can be spectacular. However, signage must not be allowed to become chaotic and unfriendly to pedestrian traffic. Nasar (1987) reports that people prefer signage with moderate rather than high complexity—measured by the amount of variation among signs in location, shape, color, direction, and lettering style. Jacobs (1993) uses Hong Kong signage as an example of complexity to the point of chaos.

The presence and activity of people add greatly to the complexity of a scene. This is true not only because people appear as discrete "objects" but because they are in constant motion. Gehl (1987, p. 25) explains that "people are attracted to other people. They gather with and move about with others and seek to place themselves near others. New activities begin in the vicinity of events that are already in progress." Allan Jacobs (1993, p. 59), in the course of his worldwide travels, found that the most popular streets were ones that contained "sidewalks fairly cluttered with humans and life," calling them "attractive obstacle courses" that never failed to entertain.

Complexity can also arise at a larger scale from the pattern of development. According to Christopher Alexander (1965), organically developed older cities have complex "semi-lattice" structures, while new planned developments have simple "tree-like structures." Integration of land uses, housing types, activities, transportation modes, and people creates diversity, and that in turn adds to complexity (Gehl 1987). Jane Jacobs (1961, p. 161) describes diversity as a mixture of commercial, residential, and civic uses in close proximity to one another, creating human traffic throughout day and night, and subsequently benefiting the safety, economic functioning, and appeal of a place.

Our expert panel related complexity to:

- layering at the edge ofstreets, from sidewalk to arcade to courtyard to building
- diversity of building ages
- diversity of social settings
- diversity of uses over the course of a day (something our videotapes could not capture).

Two panelists lamented the loss of complexity as design becomes more controlled and predictable (as in modern developments under unified ownership).

Complexity is one perceptual quality that has been measured extensively in visual assessment studies. It has been related to changes in texture, width, height, and setback of buildings (Elshestaway 1997; Stamps, Nasar, and Hanyu 2005). It has been related to building shapes, articulation, and ornamentation (Stamps 1998a, 1999; Heath, Smith, and Lim 2000).

Coherence

Coherence refers to a sense of visual order. The degree of coherence is influenced by consistency and complementarity in the scale, character, and arrangement of buildings, landscaping, street furniture, paving materials, and other physical elements.

Jacobs (1993, p. 287) describes coherence in architecture as follows: "Buildings on the best streets will get along with each other. They are not the same, but they express respect for one another, most particularly in respect to height and the way they look." According to Arnold (1993), complexity of architecture of earlier eras was given coherence by common materials, handcrafted details, and reflections of human use. Because these are absent from today's architecture, landscaping becomes critical for creating a sense of visual unity; shade trees planted close together result in an uninterrupted pattern of light and shade, unifying a scene. At the city level, coherence takes the form of orderly density patterns and hierarchies of communal spaces (Alexander, Ishikawa, and Silverstein 1977). Nikos Salingaros (2000), applying mathematical principles to the urban setting, concludes, "Geometrical coherence is an identifiable quality that ties the city together through form, and is an essential prerequisite for the vitality of the urban fabric."

Hedman (1984, p. 29) warns that when every building seeks to be a unique statement and the center of attention, there is an unexpected effect: "Instead of providing an exciting counterpoint, the addition of each new and different building intensifies the impression of a nervous, irritating confusion." He goes on to list multiple features of buildings that, when repeated, can create visual unity: building silhouettes, spacing between buildings, setbacks from the street, proportions of windows/bays/doorways, massing of building form, location of entryways, surface material and finish, shadow patterns, building scale, style of architecture, and landscaping.

While often presented as opposites, coherence and complexity represent distinct perceptual dimensions. Visual preference surveys show that viewers do not appreciate massive doses to unstructured information. People like complexity, but not the unstructured complexity of the commercial strip. Scenes with high complexity and low coherence tend to be least liked, causing Herzog, Kaplan, and Kaplan (1982, p. 59) to conclude that "high complexity urban areas must also be highly coherent." Generalizing across many surveys, Kaplan and Kaplan (1989, p. 54) deem scenes of low com-

Figures 1.7a, b, c. Video clips shot in Annapolis, MD, rating high in Coherence.

plexity and high coherence as "boring," scenes of high complexity and low coherence as "messy," but scenes of high complexity and high coherence as "rich and organized." Coherence implies not mindless repetition or blandness but, rather, continuity of design and thematic ordering.

Our expert panel described coherence in terms of repeated elements: common building masses, building setbacks, street furniture, and landscaping. They emphasized that there could be ordered diversity, and that without diversity, coherent design becomes monotonous.

Achieving coherence (often termed compatibility) may be the overriding purpose of urban design guidelines and standards. As the City of Glendale, California (2011), puts it: "The purpose of the design review process is to ensure compatibility and a level of design quality acceptable to the community."

In visual assessment studies, the coherence of scenes is frequently assessed by individual raters. The judgments tend to be very consistent and reliable across raters. Two studies have gone on to relate coherence to physical characteristics of scenes. Nasar and Stamps (2009) found that streets were rated as more coherent if infill houses had a style considered compatible with the surrounding styles (based on previous ratings of style compatibility). Streets were also rated as more coherent if the infill house was not more than roughly twice as large as other houses on the street. Previously, Nasar (1987) had found that viewers prefer street scenes with signage that is moderately complex and highly coherent. If signs have enough characteristics in common, the street scene will appear orderly, logical, and predictable to pedestrians strolling by. If not, it will appear messy.

Legibility

Legibility refers to the ease with which the spatial structure of a place can be understood and navigated as a whole. The legibility of a place is improved by a street or pedestrian network that provides travelers with a sense of orientation and relative location and by physical elements that serve as reference points.

One dictionary (American Heritage Dictionary 2006) defines legibility as "possible to read or decipher, plainly discernible, or apparent." As described by Kevin Lynch in his classic work *The Image of the City* (1960, p. 3), legibility is the apparent clarity of the cityscape, the "ease by which its parts can be recognized and can be organized into a coherent pattern." The difference between legibility and coherence, as these terms are used herein, is one of scale. Coherence refers to buildings, landscaping, street furniture, paving materials, and other physical elements that make an individual street appear orderly. Legibility refers to an orderly pattern of streets, plazas, and other large-scale elements that make a city easily understood and navigated.

Lynch suggests that when faced with a new place, people automatically create a mental map that divides the city into paths, edges, districts, nodes, and landmarks. Places with strong edges, distinct landmarks, and busy nodes allow people to form detailed and relatively accurate mental maps. Conversely, a city that has no definite edges, nodes, or visually interesting features will be difficult to make sense of and to remember. Legibility facilitates way finding, the process by which people move successfully through the physical environment to reach a desired destination, determining a route between two points, choosing an alternate route when the primary route is impassable, navigating along a route, and learning a new spatial environment.

The layout of the street network has an important influence on legibility, although the influence is sometimes ambiguous. A regular grid of streets makes it easy for people to navigate even when they are unfamiliar with a place, although it does not provide a way of distinguishing one block from another. An irregular pattern of streets, in which blocks are of irregular length and compass orientation changes from block to block, may increase the difficulty of navigating and learning the network, although it distinguishes each block with different lengths and orientations. The street network thus works together with other elements of the physical environment to determine the legibility of a place.

Figures 1.8a, b, c. Video clips shot in Charlotte, NC, rating high in Legibility.

Signage, in particular, helps to distinguish one point from another and to orient and direct a traveler through the network. Landmarks, which have an important influence on imageability, also play an important role in mental maps and thus help to increase the legibility of a place.

Visual termination and deflection points also contribute to legibility. Visual termination creates a "focal point, the vertical symbol of congregation" (Cullen 1961, p. 26). Cullen writes: "In the fertile streets . . . it is the focal point which crystallizes the situation, which confirms 'this is the spot,' 'Stop looking, it is here.'" On a large scale, visual termination points can include large civic buildings, prominent landmarks, or elements of nature. On a smaller, neighborhood scale, visual termination can be created by the use of traffic circles, bends in the roads, or other small-scale elements. Allan Jacobs (1993, p. 297) says of streets, "Since they have to start and stop somewhere, these points should be well marked." He argues that clearly marked end points both serve as reference points and give a sense of definition to an area.

Individual members of our expert panel defined legibility differently, with some positing that legibility had more to do with the context of a street than the design of the street itself, and others stating the opposite. They had difficulty distinguishing legibility from imageability, coherence, and linkage and had low inter-rater reliability in their ratings of street scenes. The one physical characteristic that came up repeatedly was the presence of marquee buildings and other landmarks.

Only one visual assessment study has attempted to measure legibility, this in connection with natural rather than urban landscapes (Herzog and Leverich 2003). Legibility was highly correlated with another perceptual quality, coherence. The hypothesized relationship to landmarks proved to be weak.

Linkage

Linkage refers to physical and visual connections from building to street, building to building, space to space, or one side of the street to the other, which tend to unify disparate elements. Tree lines, building projections, and marked crossings all create linkage.

Linkage can occur longitudinally along a street or laterally across a street. Linkages can be defined as features that promote the interconnectedness of different places and that provide convenient access between them. Linkage is closely associated with the concept of connectivity, as both are concerned with the ease of movement in an area and depend on the relationships between paths and nodes. Jacobs (1993) recommends that urban street connections occur every 300 feet at most. Alexander et al. (1977) give similar advice, suggesting pedestrian road crossings every 200 or 300 feet. They advocate the use of a separate pedestrian-only network running orthogonal to the street grid to maximize pedestrian accessibility. Duany and Plater-Zyberk (1992) generally limit the size of blocks to 230 by 600 feet to ensure reasonable travel distances. On the other hand, Appleyard (1981) argues against too much connectivity in residential areas, since through traffic can erode a sense of community, and suggests breaking up the gridiron with barriers and diverters.

Linkages between the street and surrounding buildings are also important and may be psychological as well as physical. Maintenance of sight lines and sidewalk connections are obvious ways to provide this kind of linkage, but it can also be provided in more subtle ways. For example, Arnold (1993) advocates the use of trees for linkage: continuous tree rows can psychologically connect places at either end, and tree patterns that reflect or amplify building geometry can psychologically link buildings to the street. As Trancik (1986, p. 106) puts it: "Urban design is concerned with the question of making comprehensible links between discrete things." In this way, the concept of linkage is closely related to the concept of legibility.

Figures 1.9a, b, c. Video clips shot in New York, NY, rating high in Linkage.

As with legibility, members of the expert panel had difficulty defining linkage and had low inter-rater reliability in their ratings of street scenes. Linkage was mostly defined in terms of the connectedness of things, and a grid street network was most often used to exemplify the quality of linkage.

We could find no attempts to operationalize linkage in visual assessment studies or urban design guidelines (except those relating to sidewalk connections).

Map of the Book

Measuring Urban Design presents a research-based, practical instrument and methodology for measuring the design qualities that create pedestrian-oriented urban areas. The original research discussed herein produced what is referred to as the Maryland Inventory of Urban Design Qualities (MIUDQ) protocol, as the authors were at the University of Maryland when the research was conducted.

Every operational step, from assembling an expert panel to analyzing the content of video clips, is discussed in chapter 2. We recorded video clips of streets throughout the United States—some very pleasant to walk along, others, not so much. We showed our video clips of streets to experts in the urban design field, and they spoke extensively with us about the urban design qualities they saw and about whether these streets were walkable places. We then went back and watched our video clips over and over again, noting many of the physical features (street trees, benches, storefront windows, and so on) that made up the streets we visited.

Our work then turned to objectively defining, or operationalizing, the urban design qualities that are repeatedly mentioned in classic urban design works and that our expert panel discussed extensively with us (chapter 3). Through the use of statistics, we established relationships between the physical features we observed in our video clips and the urban design qualities our experts discussed and rated as they viewed the video clips. In turn, we also established relationships between these urban design qualities and the walkability of the streets we recorded. We then used additional statistical analyses to identify urban design qualities that were rated consistently by our experts and also to identify physical features that could be measured consistently by different observers.

Next, the book illustrates a practical application of the instrument, using the example of an assessment carried out in New York City (chapter 4). This chapter was written by Dr. Kathy Neckerman, head of the Columbia

University team that performed the test; Marnie Purciel, the lead researcher; and two of their colleagues, James Quinn and Andrew Rundle. Their chapter is followed by an effort to validate the measures against pedestrian counts for the 588 New York City streets segments that were studied by Dr. Neckerman's team (chapter 5).

The end product of this effort is the field manual reproduced in chapter 6. Through the use of the manual, we believe any reader can visit a street and make the same links we discovered among physical features, urban design qualities, and walkability. The field manual provides step-by-step instructions for measuring urban design qualities, which are accompanied by extensive illustrations. We also provide a scoring sheet for easy tabulation and calculation of urban design quality scores.

In summary, *Measuring Urban Design* connects the perceptual qualities that influence walkability with practical measurement tools based on empirical research and real-world testing.

CHAPTER TWO

Data Collection

The research team on the Maryland Inventory of Urban Design Qualities (MI-UDQ) project was interdisciplinary, with members from public health as well as planning. As a result, our visual assessment study followed strict protocols to minimize the possibility of bias or inconsistency among the three principal investigators. The adherence to protocols was a novelty for the planners involved in the study, who tend to be more ad hoc in their research methods than are public health researchers. The use of hierarchical modeling methods was another innovation, learned by planners from their public health colleagues.

Expert Panel

A critical part of our work plan was to assemble a panel of urban design and planning experts. The panel members helped define perceptual qualities of urban scenes, rated different scenes with respect to these qualities in a visual assessment–style survey, submitted to interviews as they assigned their ratings to provide the research team with qualitative insights into their rating criteria, met to discuss ways of measuring perceptual qualities, and reviewed and commented on the draft field observation manual, which presented the measurement instrument in full detail. Their views on the character and importance of different urban design qualities became the gold standard for this study.

For the study, first and foremost, the panel members had to have knowledge of urban design concepts as well as expertise in urban design or related fields that would support their subjective judgments. Second, so their opinions would carry weight in the field, the panel members had to be acknowledged leaders in their respective fields. Finally, the panel members had to represent a variety of different perspectives. Having both planning and public health represented among the principal investigators ensured that different professional networks would be tapped. An effort was made to achieve a balance between urban designers and other planning professionals, and between those with a new urbanist bent (referring to a movement in design and planning that has its own design paradigm) and those with a more conventional orientation toward urban design. The panel was selected through a networking process in which the principal investigators called colleagues and asked for nominations. Experts identified in this manner were asked for additional nominations, and so the process proceeded until all ten openings were filled.

The ten expert panel members selected through this process were Victor Dover, Geoffrey Ferrell, Mark Francis, Michael Kwartler, Rob Lane, Anne Vernez Moudon, Tony Nelessen, John Peponis, Michael Southworth, and Dan Stokols (see figure 2.1). Biosketches of the expert panel members are contained in appendix 1.

Figure 2.1. Visual assessment survey during the expert panel meeting.

Videotaping

A great deal of experimentation and dialogue among the principal investigators went into developing a protocol that would mimic the experience of pedestrians. Pedestrians are usually in motion, sway a bit as they walk, have peripheral vision, and tend to scan their environments.

Three identical video camcorders were acquired so the video clips could be shot concurrently by the three co-principal investigators and research assistants in their distant geographic settings.

With five individuals shooting clips, a consistent filming protocol had to be followed to ensure that reactions to street scenes were not biased by different filming techniques. We quickly realized that much of the environment relevant to a pedestrian was not captured by stationary clips. Slow forward motion became standard despite the wobble this occasioned. The camcorder's image stabilizer helped, and both continuous and intermittent panning horizontally were tested. The continuous pan covered more ground in a given time. Vertical panning was added to approximate peripheral vision and capture vertical elements that might attract attention.

Filming was extended for longer periods so as to take in more of the street. The beginning of the block was established as the consistent starting point. We considered the possibility of continuing to film until the end of the block became visible but realized this would consume too much time on longer blocks. At some point, the wide pan to the rear was dropped as disorienting. The full pan to the right was also dropped since it brought buildings uncomfortably close.

The final filming protocol was as follows:

Have video camcorder set on high resolution. Using the "Canon Wide Attachment WA-30.5" lens and zooming out as far as possible manually, proceed as follows:

— start about 20 feet from the beginning of the block on the outside of the sidewalk

— walk slowly forward in the direction of adjacent traffic at a speed of approximately 1 mph

— as you move forward, pan slowly and continuously following the same sequence

— looking straight ahead, pan down 30 degrees, pan up 30 degrees, back to level

— pan 45 degrees right, pan up to the top of adjacent buildings or trees, and back to level

— pan 135 degrees left to the opposite side of the street, pan up to the top of opposite buildings or trees, and back to level

— pan 90 degrees right, to straight ahead

— repeat the sequence for a total of two complete pans

Library of Video Clips and Sample

Working off a shoot list, more than two hundred clips were filmed in twenty-two cities around the United States.

- In California: Walnut Creek, Berkeley, San Francisco, Woodland, Sacramento, and Davis
- In Florida: Boca Raton, Del Ray Beach, Winter Park, Fort Lauderdale, and Orlando
- In Maryland: Rockville, Annapolis, Baltimore, King Farm, and Kentlands
- In Virginia: Arlington, Herndon, and Reston
- St. Louis, Missouri
- Charlotte, North Carolina
- New York City, New York
- Nashville, Tennessee
- Washington, DC

The twenty-two cities were close to the places of work or travel for the principal investigators and their research assistants, or were visited by them on business-related travels. All scenes could be characterized as urban. All have sidewalks. All offer pedestrian amenities of some sort, such as landscaping, pedestrian lighting, street furniture, and trip destinations within view.

Diversity of street scenes was ensured by the different regional settings of the principal investigators, and the travels of principal investigators on other business during the course of the study. While they succeed to varying degrees, all streets included in the sample attempt to accommodate pedestrians.

Scenes were shot and ultimately selected for the visual assessment survey using a so-called factorial design, which captured relevant combinations of the eight urban design qualities being operationalized (tidiness was added—legibility was dropped). Without variation across the qualities, it would have been impossible to tease out the contributions of physical features to the urban design quality ratings of our expert panel.

In statistics, a full factorial design is an experiment whose design consists of two or more factors, each with discrete values or "levels" of these factors, and whose experimental units take on all possible combinations of these levels across all such factors. In this study, the factors were the urban design qualities, and the levels were our subject assessments of each scene with respect to each quality. A common experimental design is one in which all input factors are set at two levels each. In the literature, these levels are referred to as "high" and "low" or "+1" and "–1," respectively. In this study, a street scene could have high or low imageability, high or low enclosure, and so on. A design with all possible high/low combinations of all the input factors is called a full factorial design in two levels. A full factorial design would have one scene with high imageability and high enclosure, another with low imageability and low enclosure, a third high imageability and low enclosure, a fourth with low imageability and high enclosure, and so on.

If there are k factors, each at 2 levels, a full factorial design requires 2^k separate runs (in this case, the "runs" are individual video clips) to represent all possible combinations of the factors. Even if the number of factors, k, in a design is small, the 2^k runs specified for a full factorial can quickly become very large. With two levels and eight factors, a full factorial design requires 256 runs.

The solution to this problem is to use only a fraction of the runs specified by the full factorial design. In statistics, fractional factorial designs are experimental designs consisting of carefully chosen subsets (fractions) of the experimental runs of a full factorial design. The subset is chosen so as to capture the most important features of the problem studied, while using a fraction of the effort of a full factorial design in terms of experimental runs and resources. A fractional factorial design is considered a better choice when there are five or more factors, as there were in this study. The fraction may be $1/2$, $1/4$, and so forth of the runs called for by the full factorial.

To choose our samples, one principal investigator and his research assistant rated clips as high or low with respect to the eight perceptual qualities. From the larger set, thirty-two clips were selected that best matched the combinations of high/low values in a 2^{8-3} fractional factorial design. Some of clips matched high/low patterns perfectly. Others matched on only seven, six, or even five of the qualities, rather than all eight. Urban design qualities tend to covary (that is, appear in certain combinations of high and low values), making perfect matches unlikely starting with any practically sized set of clips. These carefully selected clips served as our sample in the subsequent visual assessment survey. The 2^{8-3} sample allowed us to capture the main effects of each urban design quality on overall walkability, plus two-factor interaction effects.

To expand the sample size for analytical purposes, sixteen additional clips

Table 2.1.

2^{8-4} Fractional Factorial Design That Served as a Guide to Sampling Video Clips

	Imageability	Enclosure	Human Scale	Transparency	Complexity	Coherence	Linkage	Tidiness
clip 1	low	low	low	low	low	low	low	low
clip 2	high	low	low	low	low	high	high	high
clip 3	low	high	low	low	high	low	high	high
clip 4	high	high	low	low	high	high	low	low
clip 5	low	low	high	low	high	high	high	low
clip 6	high	low	high	low	high	low	low	high
clip 7	low	high	high	low	low	high	low	high
clip 8	high	high	high	low	low	low	high	low
clip 9	low	low	low	high	high	high	low	high
clip 10	high	low	low	high	high	low	high	low
clip 11	low	high	low	high	low	high	high	low
clip 12	high	high	low	high	low	low	low	high
clip 13	low	low	high	high	low	low	high	high
clip 14	high	low	high	high	low	high	low	low
clip 15	low	high	high	high	high	low	low	low
clip 16	high	high	high	high	high	high	high	high

were later selected. For this sample, we sought to match the 2^{8-4} fractional factorial design (as shown in table 2.1).

To illustrate, we found a clip with high values of all eight urban design qualities that perfectly matched the corresponding 2^{8-4} run (clip 16 in table 2.1—shown in figure 2.2). We also found a clip that matched low values of all eight qualities (clip 1—shown in figure 2.3). But we had to settle for a clip that matched values of only seven qualities for the 2^{8-4} run that required high values of imageability, coherence, linkage, and tidiness and low values of other qualities (clip 2—shown in figure 2.4). We, again, also settled for a clip that matched only six qualities for the run that required high values for enclosure, transparency, coherence, and linkage and low values of other qualities (clip 11—shown in figure 2.5). Although we weren't able to exactly match the fractional factorial design in all cases, following the design as closely as possible resulted in the selection of clips that are distinctly different, as figures 2.2–2.5 illustrate. Where ratings for two or more clips matched factorial design equally well, clips were selected to maximize geographic diversity.

Visual Assessment Survey

The first wave of the visual assessment survey (thirty-two clips) was conducted electronically. The sample of video clips was recorded in random order onto DVDs, and the DVDs were distributed to expert panel members. A telephone survey was then conducted in which the panel member and a research team member viewed each clip concurrently, the panel member assigned scores to each clip and commented on the specific features of scenes that produced high or low scores, and the team member recorded scores and taped comments. Thus, there was a quantitative and qualitative element to the mixed-methods survey. The qualitative element would assist the research team in identifying physical features of scenes worth measuring in the subsequent content analysis and would provide a fallback for operationalizing urban design qualities if the quantitative analysis failed.

Figures 2.2a, b, c. Best matches for a run that required high values of all eight qualities.

To expand the sample, a second visual assessment survey (sixteen additional clips) was conducted face-to-face at a meeting of the expert panel. For this survey, clips were also in random order. Panel members who could not attend the meeting were sent DVDs and subsequently surveyed by phone.

Figures 2.3a, b, c. Best matches for a run that required high values of all eight qualities.

The three principal investigators and their research assistants divided up responsibility for conducting phone surveys with the expert panel members. Therefore, as with the shooting of video clips, it was necessary to establish a standard protocol for the interviews to ensure consistency and avoid possible bias in responses. Some experimentation was involved with this protocol as well.

The final protocol was as follows:

Before the interviews, contact panelists and ask them to review the scope of the project. Also ask them to have printed copies of the survey form and perceptual quality definitions available during the survey. These should be on their desks during the survey, the former to be completed and the latter as a reference. Panelists will be using their personal computers to view the DVD, and so will need hard copies of the survey form on which to record their ratings.

Begin interviews by asking if panelists have any questions or feedback on the purpose of the project, purpose of the visual assessment survey, the survey instrument itself, or the urban design qualities definitional piece. We have added still photos of scenes to the rating form. With the still photos as memory jogs, panelists can refer back to earlier clips for benchmarks as they proceed through the survey. We have also added a final column to the form, in which panelists will rate the overall quality of the walking environment for each clip.

Conduct interviews on the speaker phone, recording the entirety for later reference. An inexpensive tape recorder produces adequate sound quality. Monitor the tape recorder throughout the interview to make sure it does not run out of tape. It did so twice in our pilot session.

To show panelists the range of values represented by the sample (so they leave room for outliers at the top and bottom of the 1 to 5 scale), view clips 3, 7, 15, 16 before starting the rating process. Mention that a consistent filming protocol was used throughout which, we hope, gives them a complete picture of the streetscape. Ask them if they have any questions or feedback on the clips.

Make sure panelists have the sound on their computers turned on for the interviews. Ratings can and should be affected by sound as well as sight (so in this sense, this isn't a pure visual assessment survey).

Explain to the panelists that each clip will be played two or more times. Have them use the first pass to familiarize themselves with the scene and comment on the streetscape in open-ended fashion. On subsequent passes, have them assign quantitative ratings to all perceptual qualities on a 1–5 Likert scale. Ask them to rate in whole numbers the individual perceptual qualities, but allow them to rate with one decimal place precision on overall walkability. Make sure they provide reasons, articulate criteria, and/or define relevant physical features for each rating. One key reason per rating will be sufficient.

Concurrently, you and the panelists will play clips in the order they appear on the DVD, which was randomized. Move through the clips at panelists' desired pace. Since their comments are being tape recorded, it will not be necessary to take notes on qualitative reactions to clips. But ask panelists to give you their quantitative ratings on the second pass through each clip. You will be recording their ratings on your survey form, as they concurrently record ratings on their survey forms.

Figures 2.4a, b, c. Best matches for a run that required high values of all eight qualities.

When all 32 clips have been rated, ask them to go back on their own to finalize their ratings in light of the entire sample. Ask them to email the final rating form to you in any event, to check that you have correctly recorded ratings given over the phone. If every panelist grades harder on later clips, we can control for "order of viewing effects" statistically. If not, we will have to rely on their own adjustments upon re-viewing to achieve intra-rater reliability.

These are exceptionally knowledgeable people who will recognize many of the streets. You can confirm but don't identify places so as not to bias ratings with positive or negative associations.

Figures 2.5a, b, c. Best matches for a run that required high values of Enclosure, Transparency, Coherence, and Linkage and low values of other qualities.

CHAPTER THREE

Analysis and Final Steps

In this book, we develop a set of procedures that anyone can use to measure urban design qualities with a degree of validity and reliability. The first challenge in doing this is to explain the relationships between urban design qualities and perceived walkability and also between urban design qualities and physical features of streets. The second challenge is to demonstrate that urban design qualities can be rated consistently by different experts and that physical features can be measured consistently by different researchers. In this chapter, we use statistics to quantify both the relationships we are interested in and the reliability of our measurement methods. Urban design qualities that pass both tests are included in our field manual (chapter 6).

Walkability in Relation to Urban Design Qualities

During our visual assessment survey, we asked our expert panel to rate scenes both for walkability and also with respect to nine urban design qualities: imageability, enclosure, human scale, transparency, complexity, coherence, linkage, legibility, and tidiness. (These qualities were later narrowed down to the five qualities introduced in chapter 1: imageability, visual enclosure, human scale, transparency, and complexity. The qualities of coherence, linkage, legibility, and tidiness were dropped when it became apparent that they could not be measured or modeled reliably). These ratings became the basis for our statistical analyses.

We began by running a regression analysis using the expert panel's ratings of walkability as the dependent variable and their ratings of each urban design quality as independent variables. Using mean values for the forty-eight video clips, we found that overall walkability is directly and significantly related to each urban design quality individually. The analysis is complicated, however, by the fact that eight of the nine qualities (the exception being tidiness) are collinear. Tolerance values were unacceptably low when all variables were included in a regression at once.

Linkage and legibility appeared to be largely functions of the other urban design qualities, so they were dropped from further consideration. Of the remaining variables, human scale had the strongest relationship to overall walkability almost regardless of what combination of variables was tested. Tidiness—and to a lesser extent, transparency, enclosure, and imageability—was somewhat independent of human scale, proved significant at the 0.10 level in most model runs, and improved the explanatory power of the model (the adjusted R-squared). Coherence was ultimately dropped because it proved insignificant and reduced the adjusted R-squared of the model. Complexity was ultimately dropped even though significant in some model runs, because it altered relationships between other variables and overall walkability, and because it had a low tolerance value itself.

The best-fit equation is presented in table 3.1. Our urban design qualities explain more than 95 percent of the variation in mean overall walkability, according to our expert panel. All qualities are directly related to overall walkability, and all are significant at conventional levels, except tidiness, which falls just below the 0.10 level. Based on their t-statistics, human scale ranks first in significance as a determinant of overall walkability, imageability second, enclosure third, transparency fourth, and tidiness a distant fifth.

Table 3.1.
Regression Model for Overall Walkability

Variable	Coefficient	Standardized Coefficient	t-statistic	p-value
Constant	−0.226		−1.503	0.140
Human scale	0.411	0.420	5.814	<0.001
Transparency	0.137	0.149	2.366	0.023
Tidiness	0.070	0.059	1.598	0.117
Enclosure	0.140	0.157	2.504	0.016
Imageability	0.307	0.310	5.153	<0.001
N	48			
R-squared	.959			
Adjusted R-squared	.954			

Inter-Rater Reliability of Scene Ratings

The next step was to measure the reliability of the ratings our expert panel gave to each urban design quality. Just how reliably urban design qualities could be rated became a criterion in selecting urban design qualities to be operationalized. Various statistical techniques may be used to assess inter-rater reliability in studies like this, where multiple individuals independently rate the same set of cases. For assessing inter-rater agreement, intraclass correlation coefficients (ICCs) are more appropriate than simple correlation coefficients. Simple correlation coefficients are sensitive only to random error (chance factors), while ICCs are sensitive to both random error and systematic error (statistical bias). For example, if two experts rate a group of scenes and one of them always assigns scores that are x points higher than the other (systematic error), a simple correlation coefficient would indicate complete agreement between them. By contrast, the ICC would accurately portray the extent of disagreement between them. The ICC is the preferred measure of inter-rater reliability when cases are rated in terms of some interval variable or interval-like variable, such as the Likert scales our expert panel used to rate scenes.

The ten expert panelists independently rated each of forty-eight clips with respect to the nine urban design qualities, and values were compared for inter-rater reliability (see table 3.2). From their ICC values, most urban design

Table 3.2.

Inter-Rater Reliability for Ratings of Perceptual Qualities

	Intra-class Correlation Coefficient	95% Confidence Interval of ICC	Cronbach's Alpha
Imageability	.494	.385–.618	.930
Enclosure	.584	.478–.697	.945
Human scale	.508	.399–.630	.928
Transparency	.499	.390–.622	.926
Complexity	.508	.398–.632	.926
Coherence	.374	.271–.504	.880
Legibility	.380	.276–.509	.895
Linkage	.344	.169–.621	.896
Tidiness	.421	.314–.550	.915
N	48		

qualities demonstrate moderate inter-rater reliability among panelists (0.6 >
ICCs > 0.4); the exceptions—linkage, coherence, and legibility—show fair
reliability (0.4 > ICCs > 0.2) (Landis and Koch 1977). For purposes of comparison, Cronbach's alpha is also reported for these ratings.

Analyzing the Content of Sampled Scenes

Our analysis next turned to testing whether urban design qualities could be
explained by simple-to-measure physical features. Since our goal was to operationalize urban design qualities in objective, quantitative terms, the ratings by
the expert panel, insofar as possible, had to be explained in terms of measurable physical features of scenes. The procedural alternative to this approach—
giving users either qualitative criteria or pictorial examples upon which to base
urban design ratings—seemed fraught with subjectivity and imprecision. So
we opted for measuring physical features and relating these physical features
to our urban design quality ratings.

Urban design literature and earlier visual assessment surveys informed us
as we identified the physical features to measure. Interviews with our national expert panel proved to be very important. As panelists rated scenes,
they also commented on the physical features that caused ratings to be high
or low with respect to each urban design quality. Panelists were recorded as
they rated scenes so that we could later review recordings to identify promis-
ing variables.

The authors of this book developed a "gold standard" for the content analysis. Detailed operational rules were established for measuring each physical
feature. The features and operational definitions are listed in appendix 2. The
process might best be described as one of forced consensus. We each independently measured each feature, discussed differences, and finally reached
agreement on a single value for each physical feature of each video clip. In
this manner, all forty-eight video clips from the visual assessment survey were
analyzed for content. Physical features of each scene were quantified with as
much care and precision as the medium allowed. All told, we measured more
than one hundred features in this manner for each scene. The process typically
required more than an hour for each video clip, and much more for the more
complex scenes.

Inter-Rater Reliability of Content Analysis

Just how reliably physical features could be measured became a criterion in selecting variables for later use in operational definitions and, ultimately, in the field manual. To assess inter-rater reliability of measured physical features, a random sample of video clips was assigned to three other members of the research team. The sample consisted of twelve clips in all, or four per team member. The sample size was limited by the time required to evaluate more than one hundred features in each clip.

Before they evaluated the clips in their samples, the other team members discussed the measurement of each feature with us. As these other team members evaluated each clip in their sample, they continually referred back to the operational definitions, a process that added considerably to the time required (particularly for the researcher from public health, who had never done anything like it).

Table 3.3 lists the ICC and Chronbach's alpha values for all the physical features measured in this manner. Most features exhibited almost perfect agreement (ICCs > 0.8) or substantial agreement (0.8 > ICCs > 0.6) among the team members. It is relatively easy to count objects and measure widths. Several features had low or even negative ICC values. Of these, features such as the number of landscape elements could probably be rated more consistently with better operational definitions. Other features, such as landscape condition, involve a high degree of judgment and might require training or photographic examples to achieve reasonable inter-rater reliability. Those missing values in table 3.3 had insufficient variance across the sample to compute inter-rater reliability statistics.

Urban Design Ratings in Relation to Physical Features

At this point in our analysis, we had identified urban design qualities that are related to perceived walkability. We had also identified urban design qualities that could be rated reliably. Further, we had identified physical features that could be measured consistently. The final step was to relate physical features to the urban design ratings by the expert panel.

For this we used multivariate statistical methods. We hypothesized

Table 3.3.

Inter-Rater Reliability for Estimates of Physical Features

Variable	ICC	Alpha	Variable	ICC	Alpha	Variable	ICC	Alpha
Number of courtyards, etc.	0.471	0.611	Proportion of street wall—opposite side	0.588	0.737	Number of small planters	0.968	0.982
Arcades	—	—	Number of enclosed sides	0.389	0.640	Landscape condition	−0.115	0.244
Number of landmarks	0.763	0.878	Average building setback—same side	0.215	0.338	Common tree spacing—same side	0.766	0.867
Number of major landscape features	—	—	Common building setbacks	0.814	0.897	Common tree spacing—both sides	0.283	0.407
Memorable architecture	—	—	Building height—same side	0.741	0.864	Number of moving pedestrians	0.895	0.946
Distinctive signage	1.000	1.000	Building height to width ratio	0.855	0.940	Number of people standing	0.728	0.865
Number of long sight lines	0.585	0.714	Building height—opposite side	0.939	0.966	Number of people seated	0.994	0.997
Terminated vista	0.436	0.571	Common building heights	0.500	0.646	Noise level	0.571	0.704
Proportion of progress toward intersection	0.833	0.906	Common building masses	0.690	0.833	Outdoor dining	1.000	1.000
Proportion of progress toward distant point	0.718	0.860	Street width	0.870	0.927	Number of tables	0.916	0.954
Number of street connections	−0.110	−0.296	Median width	0.007	0.014	Number of seats	−0.052	−0.065
Number of buildings	0.913	0.951	Sidewalk width	0.693	0.807	Number of pedestrian street lights	0.938	0.967

Table 3.3. continued.

Inter-Rater Reliability for Estimates of Physical Features

Variable	ICC	Alpha	Variable	ICC	Alpha	Variable	ICC	Alpha
Number of land uses	0.762	0.852	Building height to street width ratio	0.894	0.947	Number of other pieces of street furniture	0.933	0.969
Proportion of historic buildings	0.518	0.720	Sidewalk clear width	0.506	0.690	Number of misc. street items	0.849	0.940
Number of buildings with identifiers	0.876	0.934	Buffer width	0.542	0.772	Number of pieces of public art	0.529	0.748
Proportion of buildings with ID	0.443	0.721	Number of paving materials	0.641	0.861	Number of traffic signs	0.876	0.946
Various building ages	0.845	0.916	Textured sidewalk surface	1.000	1.000	Number of place or business signs	0.761	0.865
Number of building materials	0.409	0.550	Textured street surface	1.000	1.000	Number of directional signs	0.766	0.867
Number of building colors	0.503	0.642	Pavement condition	0.627	0.771	Number of billboards	1.000	1.000
Number of accent colors	0.350	0.609	Debris condition	0.532	0.681	Common signage	—	—
Number of building projections	0.610	0.775	Number of parked cars	0.958	0.984	Graffiti	—	—
Number of visible doors	0.891	0.937	Proportion of parked cars	0.965	0.991	Proportion of sky ahead	0.831	0.899
Number of recessed doors	0.600	0.818	Number of moving cars	0.970	0.984	Proportion of buildings ahead	0.550	0.690
Proportion of recessed doors	0.531	0.790	Average speed of moving cars	0.862	0.919	Proportion of pavement ahead	0.602	0.732
Proportion of first-floor facades with windows	0.841	0.911	Number of moving cyclists	—	—	Proportion of cars ahead	0.174	0.338

Table 3.3. continued.

Inter-Rater Reliability for Estimates of Physical Features

Variable	ICC	Alpha	Variable	ICC	Alpha	Variable	ICC	Alpha
Proportion of overall façades with windows	0.643	0.764	Number of curb extensions	0.814	0.897	Proportion of street furniture ahead	0.837	0.906
Common window proportions	0.845	0.916	Number of midblock crossings	—	—	Proportion of landscaping ahead	0.911	0.949
Number of awnings or overhangs	0.717	0.828	Number of midblock pass-throughs	—	—	Proportion of sky across	0.943	0.976
Proportion of building height interruptions	-0.122	-0.064	Overhead utilities	—	—	Proportion of buildings across	0.887	0.935
Number of nonrectangular silhouettes	0.399	0.738	Number of landscape elements	-0.086	-0.019	Proportion of pavement across	0.700	0.808
Proportion of nonrectangular silhouettes	-0.040	0.251	Landscaped median	1.000	1.000	Proportion of cars across	0.939	0.967
Common architectural styles	0.431	0.675	Number of trees	0.804	0.883	Proportion of street furniture across	0.633	0.750
Common materials	0.585	0.714	Number of tree wells	0.649	0.854	Proportion of landscaping across	0.894	0.946
Proportion of active uses	0.795	0.878	Proportion of shaded sidewalk	0.922	0.956			
Proportion of street wall— same side	0.938	0.976	Number of large planters	0.349	0.510			

relationships between urban design qualities and specific physical features in order to select variables to include in our models. These hypotheses were partly a matter of common sense, partly a reflection of the urban design literature, and partly a product of the interviews with the expert panelists. To keep model building from becoming a data mining exercise, we created a matrix of hypothesized relationships and only the features plausibly linked to urban design qualities were actually tested for predictive power. Appendix 3 contains the matrix.

Cross-Classified Random Effects Models

Visual assessment studies often employ multiple regression analysis to explain scene ratings in terms of objectively measured physical features. This may not be the best approach. When ratings vary systematically by scene and by viewer, and random effects are present, the resulting data structure is best represented by a cross-classified random effects model.[1]

The dependent variable in this analysis is the urban design quality rating assigned by an individual panelist to an individual street scene. Had all forty-eight scenes been rated by all ten panelists, our sample would have consisted of 480 ratings. For one perceptual quality—linkage—one panelist declined to provide ratings for all video clips, and the sample was slightly smaller.

Ratings varied from scene to scene due to different qualities of the street itself and its edge. Ratings also varied from panelist to panelist due to differences in judgment. Some panelists were more generous in their ratings than others. Finally, ratings varied due to unique interactions between scenes and panelists. A particular scene may have evoked a particularly positive or negative reaction in a particular panelist. We viewed such unique reactions as measurement errors.

The more interesting source of variation in scores is that associated with scenes. Indeed, the purpose of this book is to identify the physical features of scenes that give rise to high or low ratings on urban design quality scales. In

---

[1] For an introduction to this class of models, we refer readers to chapter 12 in Stephen W. Raudenbush and Anthony S. Bryk, *Hierarchical Linear Models: Applications and Data Analysis Methods*, 2nd ed. (Thousand Oaks, CA: Sage, 2002).

statistical parlance, the "scene effect" gives rise to "scene variance." While not of much interest, variation also occurs across panelists and must be accounted for. Again in statistical parlance, the "viewer effect" gives rise to "viewer variance." The unique reactions of individual panelists, and the random variations in their scoring across scenes, produce "measurement error variance."

In order to bring into focus the interesting variation across street scenes, it helps statistically to separate the scene variance from viewer variance and measurement error variance. Doing so, we are able to eliminate viewer effects when evaluating the power of physical features to predict street scene ratings. If we had simply used the ratings of scenes as the dependent variable, and the physical features of scenes as explanatory variables, the effect of scene variance might have been confounded by the effect of viewer variance.

Our analysis began by partitioning the total variance in urban design quality ratings among the three sources of variation—scenes, viewers, and measurement errors. The model consisted of two parts:

actual rating = predicted rating + measurement error

where the actual rating is the sum of the predicted score for a given scene by a given viewer plus the measurement error; and

predicted rating = constant + viewer effect + scene effect

where the predicted rating is just the sum of a constant plus a viewer effect and a scene effect.

For each urban design quality, table 3.4 shows the total variance in ratings and the portions attributable to each source.[1] The fuzzier constructs, such as legibility and linkage, have higher proportions attributable to viewer judgment and measurement error.

As an example, for the urban design quality of imageability, the scene variance was 0.67, the viewer variance was 0.16, and the measurement error variance was 0.50. The total variance was thus split into the following proportions:

- 50 percent scene variance

---

[1] We used HLM 6.08, a footnotestatistical package developed by Raudenbush, Bryk, and Congdon (2004), to estimate equations.

Table 3.4.
Variance in Ratings by Source for Each Urban Design Quality (% of total variance in parentheses)

	Scene Variance	Viewer Variance	Measurement Error	Total Variance
Imageability	0.67 (50)	0.16 (12)	0.50 (38)	1.33
Enclosure	0.83 (59)	0.10 (7)	0.48 (34)	1.41
Human scale	0.68 (53)	0.11 (8)	0.50 (39)	1.29
Transparency	0.77 (51)	0.13 (8)	0.62 (41)	1.52
Complexity	0.6 (52)	0.09 (8)	0.47 (40)	1.16
Coherence	0.45 (38)	0.11 (9)	0.62 (53)	1.18
Legibility	0.46 (39)	0.17 (14)	0.55 (47)	1.18
Linkage	0.51 (34)	0.26 (17)	0.74 (39)	1.51
Tidiness	0.46 (43)	0.17 (16)	0.43 (41)	1.06

- 12 percent viewer variance
- 38 percent measurement error variance

Our analysis showed that all urban design qualities exhibit more variance across scenes than across viewers. This is not unusual in visual assessment surveys.

We estimated additional models in order to reduce the unexplained variance in urban design quality ratings. These models included characteristics of viewers and scenes:

actual rating = predicted rating + measurement error

exactly as before; and

predicted rating = constant + viewer random effect + scene random effect + a*viewer variables + b*scene variables

where the viewer random effect is the portion of the viewer effect left unexplained by viewer characteristics, the scene random effect is the portion of the scene effect left unexplained by scene characteristics, "viewer variables" is the vector of relevant viewer characteristics, "a" is the vector of associated coefficients, "scene variables" is the vector of relevant scene characteristics, and "b" is the vector of associated coefficients. These variables capture the "fixed effects" of viewers and scenes on urban design ratings.

Results of Statistical Analysis

We tested many combinations of viewer and scene variables. The only available variables characterizing viewers—urban designer or not (1 or 0 dummy) and new urbanist or not (1 or 0 dummy)—proved to have no explanatory power in most analyses. That is to say, neither variable was significant at the 0.10 probability level, except in the model for human scale, in which the variable for urban designer proved marginally significant. Apparently, urban designers and others, and new urbanists (a subset of the designers) and others, react similarly to street scenes. This is consistent with earlier visual assessment literature revealing common environmental preferences across professions.

By contrast, many of the variables characterizing scenes proved significant individually and in combination with one another. This again is consistent with the visual assessment literature. The models that reduced the unexplained variance of scores to the greatest degree, and for which all variables had the expected signs and were significant at the 0.10 level or beyond, are presented in tables 3.5 through 3.13. Most of the independent variables in these tables are object counts, though there are also dummy variables and proportions. (See appendix 2 for variable definitions.)

In all, thirty-seven physical features proved significant in one or more models. Six features were significant in two models: long sight lines, number of buildings with identifiers, proportion of first floor facade with windows, proportion of active uses, proportion of street wall—same side, and number of pieces of public art. Two features were significant in three models: number of moving pedestrians and presence of outdoor dining. The models for each quality are presented and discussed below.

Imageability

For imageability, the estimated model left the measurement error variance unchanged at 0.50, reduced the unexplained viewer variance only slightly from 0.16 to 0.15, but reduced the unexplained scene variance substantially, from

0.67 to 0.19. Altogether, 72 percent of the variation across scenes, and 37 percent of the overall variation in imageability scores (including variation across viewers and measurement errors), were explained by the significant scene variables (table 3.5). All of the significant scene variables had acceptable levels of inter-rater reliability (with intraclass correlation coefficients of 0.40 or above, except for major landscape features, which had insufficient variance across the sample to compute inter-rater reliability). The significance of the number of pedestrians and outdoor dining points to the importance of human activity in creating imageable places. The lack of significance of landmarks, memorable architecture, and public art forces us to rethink just what makes a place memorable. Overall, the model is strong.

Table 3.5.
Best-Fit Imageability Model

Variable	Coefficient	t-statistic	p-value
Constant	2.516		
Courtyards/plazas/parks (#)	0.393	3.58	0.001
Major landscape features (#)	0.735	2.00	0.046
Proportion of historic buildings	0.948	4.16	0.000
Buildings with identifiers (#)	0.115	1.80	0.072
Buildings with nonrectangular silhouettes (#)	0.0745	1.95	0.052
Pedestrians (#)	0.0271	4.73	0.000
Noise level (rating)	−0.195	−2.11	0.035
Outdoor dining (y/n)	0.703	3.97	0.000
Proportion of Scene Variance Explained	0.72		
Proportion of Total Variance Explained	0.37		

Enclosure

For enclosure, the estimated model left the measurement error variance unchanged, reduced the unexplained viewer variance slightly, from 0.10 to 0.09, and reduced the unexplained scene variance from 0.83 to 0.23. This is the largest absolute reduction in unexplained scene variance. With just five variables, the model for enclosure explains 72 percent of the scene variance and 43 percent of the total variance (table 3.6). All of the significant variables have high levels of inter-rater reliability, with ICCs above 0.59.

The signs of the coefficients in the model are as expected, with long sight lines, proportion of the view ahead that is sky, and proportion of the view across the street that is sky detracting from the perception of enclosure. A more continuous "street wall" of building facades, on each side of the street, adds to the perception of enclosure. This model suggests that enclosure is influenced not just by the near side of the street but also by views ahead and across the street. Surprisingly, the average street width, average building setback, average building height, common tree spacing and type, and relationship between the width of the street and building height were not significant. Overall, the model is strong.

Table 3.6.
Best-Fit Enclosure Model

Variable	Coefficient	t-statistic	p-value
Constant	2.570		
Long sight lines (#)	−0.308	−2.12	0.035
Proportion of street wall—same side	0.716	3.51	0.001
Proportion of street wall—opposite side	0.940	3.17	0.002
Proportion of sky ahead	−1.418	−1.92	0.055
Proportion of sky across	−2.193	−2.32	0.021
Proportion of Scene Variance Explained	0.72		
Proportion of Total Variance Explained	0.43		

Human Scale

For human scale, the estimated model left the measurement error variance unchanged, reduced the unexplained viewer variance from 0.11 to 0.08, and reduced the unexplained scene variance from 0.68 to 0.26. Seven variables explain 62 percent of the scene variance and 35 percent of the total variance in human scale (table 3.7). All of the significant variables have ICCs of 0.59 or higher. The signs of the coefficients are as expected: the number of long sight lines and building height on the same side of the street decrease the perception of human scale, while the presence of first-floor windows, small planters, and street items increase the perception of human scale. Human activities are also important, specifically the proportion of street frontage with active uses. Human scale is the only quality for which characteristics of viewers are significant:

if the viewer is an urban designer, the rating of human scale is higher, all else being equal. Overall, the model is strong.

Table 3.7.
Best-Fit Human Scale Model

Variable	Coefficient	t-statistic	p-value
Constant	2.612		
Urban designer (y/n)	0.382	1.84	0.066
Long sight lines (#)	−0.775	−4.97	0.000
Proportion of first floor with windows	0.916	2.93	0.004
Proportion of active uses	0.306	1.77	0.077
Building height (ft)	−0.00308	−2.08	0.038
Small planters (#)	0.0469	1.86	0.063
Miscellaneous street items (#)	0.0635	3.25	0.002
Proportion of Scene Variance Explained	0.62		
Proportion of Total Variance Explained	0.35		

Transparency

For transparency, the estimated model left the measurement error variance and unexplained viewer unchanged and reduced the unexplained scene variance from 0.77 to 0.29. Just three variables explain 62 percent of the scene variance and 32 percent of the total variance in transparency: the proportion of the first floor with windows, the proportion of active uses, and the proportion of street wall on the same side (table 3.8). All three variables have acceptable levels of inter-rater reliability. The model suggests that being able to see into buildings and having human activity along the street frontage both contribute to the perception of transparency. Note that windows above ground level do not increase the perception of transparency (after controlling for other variables). Overall, the model is strong.

Complexity

For complexity, the estimated model left the measurement error variance and viewer variance unchanged while reducing unexplained scene variance from 0.67 to 0.19. Six variables explain 73 percent of scene variance and 38 percent

Table 3.8.

Best-Fit Transparency Model

Variable	Coefficient	t-statistic	p-value
Constant	1.709		
Proportion of first floor with windows	1.219	3.13	0.002
Proportion of active uses	0.533	2.96	0.004
Proportion of street wall	0.666	2.57	0.011
Proportion of Scene Variance Explained	0.62		
Proportion of Total Variance Explained	0.32		

of total variance for complexity (table 3.9). Except for the number of accent colors, all variables have acceptable levels of inter-rater reliability, and the signs on the coefficients are in the expected direction. The significance of pedestrians and outdoor dining suggests that human activity may contribute as much to the perception of complexity as do physical elements. The lack of significance of several other variables is notable: number of building materials, number of building projections, textured sidewalk surfaces, and number of streetlights and other kinds of street furniture, among others. Overall, the model is strong.

Table 3.9.

Best-Fit Complexity Model

Variable	Coefficient	t-statistic	p-value
Constant	1.453		
Buildings (#)	0.0458	2.42	0.016
Dominant building colors (#)	0.225	2.74	0.007
Accent colors (#)	0.115	2.21	0.027
Pedestrians (#)	0.0311	5.96	0.000
Outdoor dining (y/n)	0.418	2.30	0.022
Public art (#)	0.286	1.96	0.051
Proportion of Scene Variance Explained	0.73		
Proportion of Total Variance Explained	0.38		

Coherence

For coherence, the estimated model left the measurement error variance and unexplained viewer variance unchanged and reduced the unexplained scene variance from 0.45 to 0.15. Only four variables were significant in the model for coherence (table 3.10). These variables explained 67 percent of the scene variance but only 25 percent of the total variance. All variables except common tree spacing have ICCs over 0.85, indicating a high degree of inter-rater reliability. Two of the variables have strong conceptual connections to coherence: common window proportions and common tree spacing and type on both sides of the street. Connections to the other two variables are less obvious. Pedestrian-scale streetlights are always of uniform style and size and unify scenes visually to a surprising degree. Pedestrians become a dominant and relatively uniform element as their numbers increase. Other conceptually important variables are missing from the model, including common architectural styles and common building masses. Overall, this model is weak.

Table 3.10.

Best-Fit Coherence Model

Variable	Coefficient	t-statistic	p-value
Constant	2.495		
Common window proportions (y/n)	0.979	6.18	0.000
Common tree spacing and type (y/n)	0.356	2.41	0.016
Pedestrians (#)	0.0217	4.29	0.000
Pedestrian-scale streetlights (#)	0.0566	1.81	0.070
Proportion of Scene Variance Explained	0.67		
Proportion of Total Variance Explained	0.25		

Legibility

For legibility, the estimated model left the measurement error variance and unexplained viewer variance unchanged (table 3.11). It reduced the unexplained scene variance from 0.46 to 0.21, accounting for only 54 percent of the scene variance and 21 percent of the total variance, the lowest percentages among the nine urban design qualities studied (refer back to table 3.4). All of the significant scene variables had acceptable levels of inter-rater reliability, except for memorable architecture, which had insufficient variance across the sample to compute inter-rater reliability. The number of buildings with identifiers and the number of signs have obvious conceptual connections to legibility; the significance of common tree spacing and memorable architecture is less easily explained but may be related to the ability to place the street in a larger spatial context. The set of variables in the model also has conceptual connections to imageability, suggesting that panelists may have had difficulty distinguishing between these two concepts. As noted earlier, legibility itself had a low level of inter-rater reliability. Overall, the model is weak.

Table 3.11.
Best-Fit Legibility Model

Variable	Coefficient	t-statistic	p-value
Constant	2.412		
Memorable architecture (y/n)	0.620	2.49	0.013
Terminated vista (y/n)	0.722	3.57	0.001
Buildings with identifiers (#)	0.228	3.55	0.001
Common tree spacing and type (y/n)	0.433	2.68	0.008
Public art (#)	0.342	2.07	0.039
Place/building/business signs (#)	0.0537	2.18	0.030
Proportion of Scene Variance Explained	0.54		
Proportion of Total Variance Explained	0.21		

Linkage

For linkage, the estimated model left the measurement error variance and unexplained viewer variance unchanged and reduced the unexplained scene variance from 0.51 to 0.20. The model for linkage, with five variables, explains 61 percent of scene variance but only 21 percent of total variance (table 3.12). Linkage has the highest viewer variance and measurement error of the nine urban design features and is tied with legibility for the smallest percentage of total variance explained. These statistics indicate lack of clarity in the concept of linkage. Four of the five variables in the model had acceptable levels of inter-rater reliability; the number of street connections to other places was the notable exception. The significance of recessed doors, outdoor dining, and common building heights on opposite sides of the street suggests the importance of psychological as well as physical connections between buildings, sidewalks, and streets. Overall, the model is weak.

Table 3.12.

Best-Fit Linkage Model

Variable	Coefficient	t-statistic	p-value
Constant	2.104		
Street connections to elsewhere (#)	0.623	3.31	0.001
Visible doors (#)	0.134	3.36	0.001
Proportion recessed doors	0.613	3.11	0.002
Common building heights (y/n)	0.576	3.52	0.001
Outdoor dining (y/n)	0.415	2.21	0.027
Proportion of Scene Variance Explained	0.61		
Proportion of Total Variance Explained	0.21		

Tidiness

For tidiness, the estimated model left the measurement error variance and un-explained viewer variance unchanged while reducing the unexplained scene variance from 0.46 to 0.14. The model for tidiness explained 70 percent of scene variance and 30 percent of total variance with just four variables (table 3.13). Two of these variables—ratings of pavement condition and debris condition—had acceptable inter-rater reliability; the rating of landscape condition did not; and the variability in overhead utilities was not large enough to compute inter-rater reliability. The coefficients of all explanatory variables have the expected signs, and the variables are those with the strongest conceptual connections to tidiness. Overall, the model is strong, although inter-rater reliability for landscape condition is a concern.

Table 3.13.

Best-Fit Tidiness Model

Variable	Coefficient	t-statistic	p-value
Pavement condition (rating)	0.197	3.31	0.001
Debris condition (rating)	0.272	3.84	0.000
Overhead utilities (y/n)	−0.638	−2.34	0.020
Landscape condition (rating)	0.230	4.29	0.000
Proportion of Scene Variance Explained	0.70		
Proportion of Total Variance Explained	0.30		

Final Steps

Through the course of the study, it became clear that not all urban design qualities could be defined operationally. Some are clearly more amenable to measurement than are others. To decide which urban design qualities would be operationalized in the field survey instrument, five criteria were established:

1. The urban design quality was rated by the expert panel with at least a moderate degree of inter-rater reliability (ICC > 0.4), following the criteria suggested by Landis and Koch (1977).
2. The total variance in ratings of the urban design quality was explained to at least a moderate degree by measurable physical features of scenes (explained portion > 0.3).
3. The portion of total variance in ratings attributable to scenes was explained to a substantial degree by measurable physical features of scenes (explained portion > 0.6).
4. All physical features related to ratings of a particular urban design quality were measured by the research team with at least a moderate degree of inter-rater reliability (ICC > 0.4), excluding those for which ICC values could not be computed because of insufficient variation in that quality across sampled scenes.
5. The urban design quality as judged by the expert panel had a statistically significant relationship to overall walkability ratings by the expert panel (p < 0.05).

According to our criteria, the qualities of imageability, enclosure, human scale, and transparency had great potential for operationalization (see table 3.14). They met all five criteria. The qualities of legibility, linkage, and coherence had very little potential for operationalization, with each meeting only one of five criteria. They were given no further consideration. The qualities of complexity and tidiness fell somewhere between the extremes, meeting three of five criteria; tidiness came close to meeting a fourth.

A draft field survey instrument was prepared for the six remaining urban design qualities:

- imageability

- enclosure
- human scale
- transparency
- complexity
- tidiness

The draft instrument showed users how to measure physical features related to each of these qualities and how to convert these measurements into urban design quality scores based on the statistical models described earlier in this chapter.

Table 3.14.

Performance of Urban Design Qualities Relative to Selection Criteria

	Inter-Rater Reliability of Rating of Quality (ICC)	Portion of Scene Variance/Total Variance Explained by Best-Fit Models	Inter-Rater Reliability of Significant Variables (no. with ICC>0.4)	Relationship to Walkability in Best-Fit Model (p-value)	Criteria Met
Imageability	0.494	0.72/0.37	7 of 7 (1 missing)	<0.001	5 of 5
Legibility	0.380	0.54/0.21	5 of 5 (1 missing)	—	1 of 5
Enclosure	0.584	0.72/0.43	5 of 5	0.016	5 of 5
Human scale	0.508	0.62/0.35	7 of 7	<0.001	5 of 5
Transparency	0.499	0.62/0.32	3 of 3	0.023	5 of 5
Linkage	0.344	0.61/0.21	4 of 5	—	1 of 5
Complexity	0.508	0.73/0.38	5 of 6	—	3 of 5
Coherence	0.374	0.67/0.25	3 of 4	—	1 of 5
Tidiness	0.421	0.70/0.30	2 of 3 (1 missing)	0.117	3 of 5

Test and Refine the Draft Instrument

With the draft instrument in hand, the authors went into the field with University of Maryland graduate students to test measurement protocols. Scenes that were part of the original visual assessment survey were used to assess whether measurements of physical features in the field were consistent with measurements in the lab using video clips. We were attempting to validate the use of video clips in our earlier urban design quality analyses. We were also seeing how the protocol used to shoot clips would translate into a procedure for field measurements.

In the field, we measured all physical features that proved significant contributors to the remaining six urban design qualities. We did this for a sample of sixteen street scenes from our original set of forty-eight scenes. Resulting field measurements were compared to our gold standard estimates based on video clips. Field observations and video clips were compared for the following: (1) inter-rater reliability of individual measurements; (2) inter-rater reliability of urban design quality scores based on the individual measurements; (3) rank-order correlations of individual measurements (assuming that relative ranking of scenes might be comparable even if absolute values differ between field observations and video clips); and (4) rank-order correlations of urban design quality scores (assuming again that relative rankings might be comparable even if absolute values differ).

What we found were major discrepancies between measurements in the field and the lab for certain physical features, and hence significant discrepancies for the urban design qualities to which they contribute in our scoring formulas. Discrepancies were significant for the following qualities and contributing features (the latter in parentheses):

- imageability (number of buildings with identifiers and noise level)
- enclosure (number of long sight lines and proportion of sky across the street)
- human scale (number of long sight lines)
- complexity (number of primary building colors and number of accent colors)

The time between the filming of video clips and the field validation accounted for some of the discrepancies. More than a year had passed, and validations often occurred at a different time of day, day of the week, and season of the year. Figure 3.1 (a–c) compares one scene at the time of original filming to the same scene at the time of field validation. Occurring after a long winter, the validation process found many streets stark, depopulated, and in need of maintenance.

Other discrepancies arose from the greater distance observers could travel in about the same time when simply walking rather than shooting video clips.

Count totals tended to be higher in the field than in the lab because the field survey protocol took observers farther down the block. For some scenes, counts were much higher. For others, they were only marginally so.

Still other discrepancies were inherent in the medium used in the lab, that is, in the video clips themselves. Shadows, glare, and panning limited what could be seen in the clips, particularly on the opposite side of the street and ahead in the distance. We could not read signs across the street. We could not distinguish different shades of colors. We could not see buildings in the distance.

To deal with discrepancies, we had four options: (1) ignore them on the assumption that the relationships between urban design qualities and physical features are as estimated from the clips, even if measurements differ; (2) refine field measurement protocols to more closely approximate measurements based on clips; (3) drop physical features that could not be measured consistently in the field and re-estimate the models without these features; or (4) drop urban design qualities that could not be estimated consistently due to inconsistent measures of component physical features.

Option 4 was the only reasonable choice for one urban design quality, tidiness. Two of the component variables—debris condition and landscape condition—were judged to be too variable over time and too subjectively assessed by different observers. Field and lab

Figures 3.1a, b. Original video clips of a street scene used in developing perceptual quality models.

Figure 3.1c. The same street scene during field validation.

estimates of tidiness were inconsistent even as measured by the Spearman rank-order correlation coefficient.

Option 2 was preferred in other cases. For certain features, changes in measurement protocols were implemented through changes in the field survey instrument. Number of building colors, for example, could be estimated more consistently by instructing users to count only the number of basic colors, not shadings. Noise levels could be estimated more consistently by instructing users to average noise levels over several passes of the study area.

For two features, field experience taught us to combine elements treated separately in our original analyses. The distinction between people walking, standing, and sitting struck us as artificial when we walked the same stretch of street several times. Walkers became standers and so forth. The distinction among the different categories of street furniture and miscellaneous street items was difficult to keep straight. Parking meters and trash cans were in one category; hydrants and ATMs, in another. Tables, seating, and streetlights were in a third, fourth, and fifth category. So we decided to combine categories and test the resulting variables in our urban design quality models.

The combined variable "people" within a scene was substituted for "moving pedestrians" in the models of imageability and complexity. It had a slightly higher significance level in the imageability model, without greatly affecting the relationship of other variables to imageability ratings. It did not perform as well as moving pedestrians in the complexity model.

The combined variable "all street furniture and other street items" was substituted for "miscellaneous street items" in the model of human scale. This variable is the sum of the number of tables, number of seats, number of pedestrian-scale streetlights, number of pieces of other street furniture, and number of miscellaneous street items. It improved the overall explanatory power of the human-scale model and caused one of the variables that had been significant—proportion of active uses along the street—to no longer be so. The proportion of active uses is highly correlated with the new combined "all street furniture and other street items" variable. The new combined variable was also tested in the complexity model and proved insignificant.

The field survey instrument was revised to reflect these changes. The final instrument is presented in chapter 6. Each urban design quality is presented with a set of instructions. All of the instructions follow the same format. The first page of instructions introduces users to the urban design quality. The next few pages show users how to measure the urban design quality. The last page provides a scoring sheet that can be used in the field to record measurements and calculate urban design quality scores for the street segment in question.

Train Raters in the Classroom

With the final field survey instrument in hand, students from UC Davis were given classroom training in its use. The classroom training took three hours. Eight students participated in the training.

The protocol for the classroom training was as follows:

Step 1. Review the field survey instrument.
Trainees were given copies of the field survey instrument and were introduced to its contents. For each urban design quality, the component physical features were reviewed and the measurement protocols were described. Trainees were shown scoring sheets at the end of the instrument. They were encouraged to ask questions.

Step 2. Review the gold standard measurements for the test clips.
A video clip from the original expert panel visual assessment survey was shown to trainees using a DVD and digital projector. The first scoring sheet was filled out with the authors' gold standard measurements. For each physical feature on the scoring sheet, the gold standard measurement was reviewed as the clip was played. The clip was replayed as many times as required to review all physical features on the scoring sheet. The gold standard measurements were presented not as hard and fast but, rather, only as values arrived at through a careful process.

Step 3. Make independent measurements for additional test clips.
For another video clip, trainees made measurements on their own, filling out a blank scoring sheet as they went along. The clip was replayed as many times as required for them to complete the task. When all trainees were done, the trainer read, and the trainees recorded, the gold standard measurements next to the trainees' own measurements. The clip was then reviewed to reconcile differences in measurements. Again, gold standard measurements were not presented as indisputable. Much time was spent discussing differences. This process was repeated with additional clips until all trainees, in a show of hands, expressed confidence in their ability to measure physical features of scenes consistently.

Field-Test the Survey Instrument

After the UC Davis students were trained in the classroom, they were sent into the field to complete observations for selected street segments. Ten segments in downtown Davis, California, and six segments in downtown Sacramento, California, were used in this field test. These segments were chosen to achieve as much variation as possible in the measured qualities. Two students were assigned to each segment to enable an analysis of inter-rater reliability. A total of thirty-two observations were thus completed. Raters were debriefed after completing their observations and provided suggestions for clarifying the field instrument.

ICC and Chronbach's alpha values for physical features and for urban design quality scores are presented in table 3.15. For half of the features, there was almost perfect agreement (ICCs > 0.8) or substantial agreement (0.8 > ICCs > 0.6) between the raters. For four more features, there was good agreement (0.6 > ICCs > 0.4).

For seven features, agreement was fair or poor for a variety of possible reasons:

- *Long sight lines*. There was very little variation in the measurements of this feature. Only four values are possible, and none of the test segments had more than two long sight lines. Still, the disagreement between raters was often large: on five segments, one rater indicated zero sight lines while the other rater indicated two sight lines. As a result, we modified the instructional language in the field instrument.
- *Street wall*. The poor results for street wall were influenced by two segments in particular. On one segment, a five-story parking garage abutted the sidewalk, although the ground floor was set back several feet. On another segment, several detached buildings were set back several feet from the sidewalk. In both cases, the raters made different decisions about whether to count the buildings as a part of the street wall. With these two segments removed, the ICC for this feature was 0.605. The field instrument was edited to more clearly specify which buildings contribute to the street wall.
- *Sky ahead and sky across*. Raters found these measurements difficult to estimate in the field, although they were relatively easy to estimate

Table 3.15.

Field Test Results

	Alpha	ICC
Imageability	0.927	0.863
1. Number of courtyards, plazas, and parks (both sides)	0.845	0.584
2. Number of major landscape features (both sides, beyond study area)	n/a	n/a
3. Proportion of historic building frontage (both sides, within study area)	0.750	0.864
4. Number of buildings with identifiers (both sides, within study area)	0.875	0.769
5. Number of buildings with nonrectangular shapes (both sides)	0.899	0.818
6. Presence of outdoor dining (your side, within study area)	0.887	0.809
7. Number of pedestrians (your side, within study area)	0.960	0.913
8. Noise level (both sides, within study area)	0.618	0.432
Enclosure	0.232	0.033
1. Number of long sight lines (both sides, beyond study area)	−0.208	−0.238
2a. Proportion of street wall (your side, beyond study area)	0.517	0.373
2b. Proportion of street wall (opposite side, beyond study area)	0.863	0.725
3a. Proportion of sky (ahead, beyond study area)	0.330	0.157
3b. Proportion of sky (across, beyond study area)	−0.568	−0.208
Human Scale	0.768	0.491
1. Number of long sight lines (both sides, beyond study area)	−0.208	−0.238
2. Proportion of windows at street level (your side, within study area)	0.798	0.663
3. Proportion of active uses (your side, within study area)	0.422	0.239
4. Average building heights (your side, within study area)	0.956	0.912
5. Number of small planters (your side, within study area)	0.786	0.622
6. Number of miscellaneous street items (your side, within study area)	0.547	0.422
Transparency	0.817	0.708
1. Proportion of windows at street level (your side, within study area)	0.798	0.663
2. Proportion of street wall (your side, beyond study area)	0.517	0.373
3. Proportion of active uses (your side, within study area)	0.422	0.239
Complexity	0.868	0.780
1. Number of buildings (both sides, beyond study area)	0.592	0.388
2a. Number of primary building colors (both sides, beyond study area)	0.279	0.188
2b. Number of accent colors (both sides, beyond study area)	0.551	0.331
3. Presence of outdoor dining (your side, within study area)	0.887	0.809
4. Number of pieces of public art (both sides, within study area)	0.677	0.528
5. Number of pedestrians (your side, within study area)	0.836	0.700

from the video clips. Differences between the raters stemmed from differences in the choice of exact location from which to estimate proportion of sky and difficulty in judging the extent of their field of vision. The field instrument now suggests the use of a cardboard frame to ensure consistency.

- *Active uses.* The poor results for this feature are related to the poor results for street walls. Because raters made different judgments about which buildings fronted on the street, they came up with different proportions of buildings with active uses. When the two problematic segments were excluded from the analysis, the ICC increased to 0.562.
- *Number of buildings.* The results for this feature were fair. Large differences for one segment can be explained by differences in the interpretation of which buildings were visible enough to be counted. With the problematic segment excluded from the analysis, the ICC increased to 0.685.
- *Basic colors and accent colors.* The poor results for these features can be partly explained by the low variation. However, the measurements for these features were inconsistent for most segments. Raters differed in their judgment of whether two colors were sufficiently different to count as two colors; tans, grays, and other neutrals seemed particularly challenging.

Among the urban design qualities, imageability had the highest reliability, closely followed by complexity and transparency. The reliability for human scale was lower but still good. However, the reliability for enclosure was poor, given the poor reliability for sight lines, sky ahead, and sky across. Improvements in reliability for these features would improve the reliability of enclosure measurements.

Based on these results and the comments and suggestions of the raters, several refinements were made to the field instrument. Although the final version of the field instrument was not retested for inter-rater reliability, we believe that the refinements improved reliability. In addition, a longer classroom training session that focuses on the problematic features should help to increase inter-rater reliability.

CHAPTER FOUR

Urban Design Qualities for New York City

Kathryn M. Neckerman, Marnie Purciel-Hill,
James W. Quinn, and Andrew Rundle

In 2006, with support from the Robert Wood Johnson Foundation (RWJF) Active Living Research program, researchers at Columbia University sampled 588 block faces in New York City and sent a team of observers to collect data on these locations using the Maryland Inventory of Urban Design Qualities (MIUDQ) protocol. The study was conceived and carried out by Columbia's Built Environment and Health (BEH) group, an interdisciplinary group of researchers who study the ways that neighborhood physical and social environments shape health behaviors and outcomes.[1] To our knowledge, this is the largest-scale implementation of the MIUDQ instrument that has been conducted so far.

This chapter describes the results of the study. After briefly presenting the background, the chapter discusses the procedures used to collect urban design data; presents descriptive results for imageability, enclosure, human scale, transparency, and complexity in New York City; and considers how these urban design qualities vary across the city. It summarizes differences in urban design scores across New York City's five boroughs and examines the extent to which these scores vary systematically by neighborhood age, urban form, and income. The chapter closes with a discussion of new research that extends this work by implementing the MIUDQ in new formats.

[1] Funding for this study was provided by Robert Wood Johnson Foundation Active Living Research grant #58089. The research was also supported by awards from the National Institute of Environmental Health Sciences (R01ES014229) and the National Institute of Child Health and Human Development (R21HD062965), and by the Robert Wood Johnson Foundation Health & Society Scholars program at Columbia University. The field team included Catherine Chong, Silvett Garcia, Jits Gysen, Victoria Lowerson, Joshua Margul, and Ellen Marrone. Ellen Marrone also helped with development of the field manual.

Background

Architects and urban planners have written extensively about the human response to the built environment (Cullen 1961; Alexander et al. 1977; Whyte 1980; Gehl 1987; Jacobs and Appleyard 1987; Rapoport 1990; Arnold 1993; Jacobs 1993). In his classic book *The Image of the City* (1960), for instance, Lynch argues that distinctive buildings or landscape features promote a vivid and memorable sense of place and help people orient themselves within the built environment; this imageability makes a place more comfortable and rewarding in which to walk. Enclosure—the quality of a well-defined and room-like outdoor space—is said to make people feel more safe. Human-scale spaces may be less intimidating than those built on a larger scale; similarly, "transparent" spaces, in which human activity beyond the street wall is visible or at least implied, may promote a sense of intimacy and connection. Complexity—a density of visual detail—makes a street scene more stimulating to pedestrians moving through the environment (Rapoport 1977).

Over the last decade and a half, health researchers have become interested in the built environment as an influence on health behaviors, including physical activity. A great deal of this work has focused either on walkable urban form—characteristics such as population density or land use mix that are believed to promote active transportation—or on parks and other venues for recreational physical activity (Brownson et al. 2009). From this start, however, urban planners and architects participated in this research and made the case that aesthetically appealing environments could make walking rewarding in and of itself (Handy et al. 2002). Reflecting this perspective in an influential conceptual discussion of the built environment, Pikora and colleagues (2003, p. 1696) observed that urban design properties such as "the diversity and interest of . . . architectural designs within the neighborhood" might promote pedestrian activity.

Yet empirical tests of this idea remain limited. Although the literature in architecture, planning, and environmental psychology is peppered with empirical studies of how individuals perceive and respond to urban design qualities (Lynch 1960; Whyte 1980; Appleyard 1981; Stamps 1998a), validated urban design measures were seldom available for use in large-scale studies of health. Epidemiological research that incorporates an aesthetic dimension has focused primarily on green space such as parks or natural areas or on physical disorder (e.g., deteriorated buildings, graffiti) rather than on features of architecture and site design (Ball et al. 2001; Giles-Corti and Donovan 2002, 2003; Brownson et al. 2004; Humpel et al. 2004). Studies that conceptualize neighborhood aesthetics more broadly, considering qualities such as attractive or interesting views, generally rely on respondent self-report (Ball et al. 2001; Carnegie et al. 2002; Giles-Corti and Donovan 2002, 2003; Eyler et al. 2003; Humpel et al. 2004). Few studies have been able to draw on objective measures of neighborhood aesthetics that tap properties besides natural features and physical disorder (Lovasi et al. 2012).

The MIUDQ offers researchers a "gold standard" for the systematic measurement of urban design and motivated our decision to implement it in New York City (NYC). The NYC application of the MIUDQ provided the opportunity to develop measures of urban design in a large-scale study relating the built environment to health outcomes.

Neighborhood Characteristics and Urban Design

Having a sample of blocks from all over the city allowed us to consider whether urban design properties are associated systematically with neighborhood characteristics. We expected that urban design might be patterned by three kinds of neighborhood characteristics: age, urban form, and income. Our expectations about these relationships are summarized in table 4.1 and discussed below.

Table 4.1.

Predicted Relationships between Neighborhood Characteristics and Urban Design Qualities

	Imageability	Enclosure	Human Scale	Transparency	Complexity
Newer housing	−	−	−	−	−
Population density	+	+	−	+	+
% commercial	+	?	+	+	+
Median income	+	+	+	+	+

Note: "+" indicates a positive association. "−" indicates a negative association. "?" indicates no prediction about direction of association.

Neighborhood Age

The age of a neighborhood's housing stock is likely to be associated with measures of urban design because buildings tend to reflect the architectural styles of the era in which they were built. "Prewar" buildings (constructed before 1940) typically have more ornamentation than those constructed later. The modernist and international styles popular in the period between 1940 and 1970 are known for their simple, functionalist forms. More recently, buildings in the postmodern style reintroduced some ornament (and sometimes color), incorporating references to an eclectic array of traditional styles; most such buildings, however, remain plainer than prewar structures.

In addition, neighborhood age can shape urban design because building size and street design reflect the building and transportation technologies of the time they were built. The development of the elevator and of steel-framed structures allowed the construction of taller buildings, while the increasing use of the private automobile allowed lower-density development and was often associated with deep setbacks from the street to accommodate parking lots in front of commercial and institutional buildings.

We expected that "younger" neighborhoods—those with more recently constructed housing—would have lower imageability scores because historic building frontage is itself an indicator for imageability, and because the older, more ornamented architectural styles are more likely to appear nonrectangular (also an indicator for imageability). Younger neighborhoods are also less likely to have a street wall, because they tend to have lower-density construction and deeper setbacks; for this reason, their enclosure and transparency scores are likely to be lower. If newer buildings are taller, the block may score lower for human scale. Younger neighborhoods may score lower on complexity, partly because new building technologies allow larger—and thus fewer—buildings per block face, and partly because the modernist architectural style tends to be relatively austere and monochromatic and thus to have fewer base and accent colors.

Urban Form

We expected measures of urban form, specifically population density and land use mix, to be associated with urban design. High population density is likely to generate more pedestrian traffic; the number of pedestrians observed on the street is one indicator of imageability and complexity. In addition, it is likely to be associated with shorter setbacks and taller buildings, simply because more built space is required to accommodate a more densely settled population; higher scores on enclosure and transparency are likely to result. On the other hand, population density may have a negative association with human scale if it is associated with more massive buildings.

Land use mix, in particular the mix of residential and commercial uses, is also likely to be associated with urban design. Mixed-use areas are likely to have more daytime pedestrian traffic than those that are only residential, raising scores for imageability and complexity. In addition, areas zoned for commercial land use are more likely to have outdoor cafés, buildings with identifiers, buildings with active uses, and a higher proportion of the street segment with windows; these items include indicators for imageability, human scale, transparency, and complexity.

Median Income

Lastly, we expected higher-income neighborhoods to have higher urban design scores. If these attributes are indeed attractive, then we would expect them to be capitalized into the price of housing: houses and apartments in neighborhoods with high imageability, enclosure, and so on should be more expensive, all else equal, and would attract relatively affluent residents. In addition, amenities such as outdoor dining are likely to be more common in neighborhoods whose residents have more discretionary income. Our group conducted a field study in New York City that compared high- and low-poverty neighborhoods (with poverty rates above and below 20 percent) that were matched in terms of their walkability scores and found that blocks in low-poverty neighborhoods were more likely to contain landmarked buildings, outdoor cafés, ornate or decorative architecture, and sidewalk conveniences (e.g., ATMs, mailboxes) and less likely to have excessive noise (Neckerman et al. 2009).

In addition, a neighborhood's median income may be associated with urban design because much of the city's public or subsidized housing for low-income residents, built between about 1945 and 1970, reflects a specific set of design ideas (von Hoffman 1996). These housing developments were characteristically high-rise structures with minimal ornamentation. Often, they were set back from the street in courtyards or open areas—a design sometimes described as "tower in the park." In some cases, streets were demapped and commercial activity excluded in order to isolate the housing from adjacent slum areas. Similar design principles were applied in some large-scale housing developments for moderate-income residents, such as Co-op City in the Bronx and Stuyvesant Town in Manhattan. Such housing developments, found more often in low- to moderate-income neighborhoods, are likely to have lower scores for historic building frontage, buildings with identifiers, nonrectangular shapes, proportion with street wall, number of buildings, and variety of building colors, as well as higher average height. As a result, we expect blocks in these less affluent neighborhoods to have lower scores on all five urban design properties.

Methods

Data on urban design in New York City were collected by a field team of six student interns who audited a total of 588 block faces. This section describes procedures for sampling block faces and for collecting the data. It also discusses the analyses relating neighborhood characteristics to urban design qualities.

Block Face Sample

Our sample of block faces was selected via a multistep procedure intended both to reflect New York City's diversity and to reduce the burden of travel between sites for the observers. We sampled blocks from six strata representing two dimensions—building density and land use—using New York City's Primary Land Use Tax Output database (PLUTO), a tax lot database, to define the strata. The 2,216 census tracts in New York City were categorized as low or high on building floor density (the ratio of total floor area to total tax parcel area) and as low, medium, or high on the proportion of floor area in the tract devoted to residential versus all other land uses (see table 4.2). To reduce travel time between the blocks selected for observation, we limited the number of tracts from which blocks would be selected: 175 tracts were selected from each of the six cells, for a total of 1,050 tracts. Finally, 600 blocks (100 from each cell) were randomly selected from the blocks contained within these 1,050 tracts.

Table 4.2.

Sampling Strata

Building Floor Density	% Residential Floor Area		
	Low	Medium	High
Low	175 tracts, 100 blocks	175 tracts, 100 blocks	175 tracts, 100 blocks
High	175 tracts, 100 blocks	175 tracts, 100 blocks	175 tracts, 100 blocks

To create the blocks used for sampling, tax lots from PLUTO were aggregated up to the block level in order to more closely represent the arrangement of developed land, curb lines, and streets. Once these blocks were selected, block polygons were converted to line files and split into the individual lines that make up the separate faces of the block. Further editing of the block face line file was necessary to create observable block faces. An observable block face was defined as not longer than 800 feet (generally the length of a long block in Manhattan), no shorter than 200 feet long (generally the length of a short block in Manhattan), and coinciding with an apparent starting place on the block. Block face lines were selected by randomly assigning first a "1" to one of the block face lines on each of the 600 blocks, then a "2" to the next block face line (of the remaining lines) on each block, then a "3," and so forth. Observers used this randomly assigned sequence in the field when the first block face was not physically accessible or did not meet the observable requirements: if block face 1 was not observable, the coder moved on to block face 2. The final sample included 588 block faces, which are mapped in figure 4.1.

Training and Field Procedures

Before beginning the training, we reviewed the field manual and scoring instrument prepared by the Ewing team (see chapter 6) and scored several nearby block faces to identify ways the manual might be adapted for use in New York City. The field manual we used was based on the Ewing team's work but included pictures, questions, and distinctions relevant to the New York City setting.

The fieldwork, supported by funding from the RWJF Active Living Research program and by the summer intern program at Columbia's Institute for

Figure 4.1. Location of audited block faces.

Social and Economic Research and Policy, was conducted in the summer of 2006 by six student interns. These interns took part in a two-and-a-half-day training that included an introduction to the five urban design qualities and the physical features by which each was measured. The interns viewed and coded video clips (provided by the Ewing team) and then reviewed and discussed their coding results compared with the gold standard codes provided by the Ewing team. All six interns then coded several blocks together with the field coordinator present to further align scoring decisions. On the latter part of the second day, observers conducted preliminary fieldwork in teams, the results of which were reviewed by the group the next day. This exercise provided each observer with the benefit of the experience of the entire group and prevented coding inconsistencies later on. Questions that arose early in the fieldwork were incorporated into an addendum to the manual.

On average, auditing one block face took about twenty minutes. Observers, who were usually sent out in pairs, traveled to most sites via public transit; the field team also spent a few days traveling by car to areas that were less accessible by transit. Block faces in close proximity were grouped together or along transit routes to reduce travel time.

Reliability

A few items remained difficult for coders, including the challenges of counting people on very busy streets and determining what constitutes a rectangular versus a nonrectangular building, what qualifies as street furniture (and whether to set a maximum for this count), how to classify construction sites, and how to count building and accent colors (e.g., at what point are variations in shade different enough to count as two different colors?).

Overall, however, the measures were implemented with a high degree of consistency across coders. To assess inter-rater reliability, thirteen block faces were scored independently by all six raters and inter-class correlation coefficients (ICCs) were computed for each urban design quality and each rater. The resulting ICCs for imageability (0.72), enclosure (0.81), human scale (0.70), transparency (0.96), and complexity (0.79) were all in the good to excellent range.

Neighborhood Measures and Statistical Analyses

After calculating descriptive statistics for the five urban design qualities and for individual items, we conducted a series of multivariable OLS (ordinary least squares) regressions that relate neighborhood characteristics to urban design in New York City. To evaluate the associations between urban design qualities and neighborhood age, urban form, and median income, we matched the 588 blocks in our sample to census tract–level characteristics from the 2000 Census sf3 and to an indicator derived from the NYC PLUTO database. The measure of neighborhood age is based on the census measures of the year in which residential structures were built. We constructed a single measure of the proportions of housing units in the tract that were built after 1939; to provide more detail, an alternative specification included measures of the proportion of housing units built in 1940–1949, 1950–1959, 1960–1969, and 1970–2000. To measure urban form, we included the natural log of the census-based measure of population density. The tract-level measure of commercial land use was derived from the NYC PLUTO data set; it represents the proportion of floor area across all buildings in the tract that is classified as having a commercial land use. (In an alternative set of analyses, we substituted an entropy measure that ranged from 0 for tracts including residential but no commercial uses or commercial but no residential, to 1 for tracts in which residential and commercial land uses were represented equally. This measure is theoretically less satisfactory because exclusively residential and exclusively commercial areas are assigned the same code; in our analyses, it had no statistically significant associations with any of the urban design qualities.) Median household income for the tract was drawn from the 2000 census; in the regression analyses, we rescaled the variable, dividing it by 1,000. Six blocks were located in tracts with no residential population and were excluded from the analysis. All analyses also included indicators for the borough in which each block was located.

We conducted two sets of multivariate analyses. The first examines the associations between tract-level neighborhood characteristics and the five urban design qualities. The second describes differences in urban design across the five boroughs and examines whether these differences remain after adjustment for indicators of neighborhood age, urban form, and income.

Results

Table 4.3 displays means, standard deviations, and medians for the five urban design measures, along with descriptive characteristics for the component measures. For many of the individual items, the median is substantially below the mean, suggesting a distribution skewed to the right. The combined urban design quality scores, however, were more normally distributed; skewness statistics for these scores ranged from –0.855 to 1.202.

Blocks that scored well on one urban design measure tended to have relatively high scores on other measures as well. Table 4.4 displays correlation coefficients for the five characteristics. All correlations were positive although they varied considerably in size, ranging from 0.092 (imageability and

Table 4.3.

Mean, Standard Deviation, and Median for Urban Design Qualities and Individual Items for 588 Block Faces in New York City

Urban Design Qualities and Individual Items	Mean	SD	Median
Imageability	3.58	1.01	3.37
Number of courtyards, plazas, and parks on the block face	0.25	0.62	0
Number of major landscape features visible from the block face	0.02	0.15	0
Proportion of historic building frontage (both sides)	0.22	0.31	0
Number of buildings with identifiers (both sides)	2.46	3.52	1
Number of buildings with nonrectangular shapes (both sides)	9.52	10.73	6
Presence of outdoor dining (observer side)	0.01	0.11	0
Number of people (observer side)	5.64	12.98	2
Noise level	2.05	0.84	2
Enclosure	3.06	0.75	3.14
Number of long sight lines visible in three directions	0.40	0.55	0
Proportion of street segment with street wall (observer side)	0.57	0.36	0.6
Proportion of street segment with street wall (opposite side of street)	0.55	0.38	0.65
Proportion of the sky visible straight ahead	0.12	0.15	0.05
Proportion of the sky visible looking across the street	0.07	0.15	0
Human Scale	2.93	0.79	2.83
Number of long sight lines visible in three directions	0.40	0.55	0
Proportion of street segment with windows (observer side first floor)	0.24	0.24	0.2
Average height of buildings weighted by building frontage (observer side)	39.93	50.95	24
Number of small planters (observer side)	5.48	10.43	0
Number of pieces of street furniture (observer side)	5.55	6.96	3
Transparency	2.66	0.57	2.56
Proportion of street segment with windows (observer side first floor)	0.24	0.24	0.2
Proportion of street segment with street wall (observer side)	0.57	0.36	0.6
Proportion of street segment with active uses (observer side)	0.54	0.39	0.6
Complexity	4.81	1.05	4.66
Number of buildings (both sides)	13.27	11.85	9
Number of basic building colors (both sides)	3.32	1.70	3
Number of accent building colors (both sides)	4.86	2.05	5
Presence of outdoor dining (observer side)	0.01	0.11	0
Number of pieces of public art (both sides)	0.06	0.44	0
Number of people (observer side)	5.64	12.98	2

Table 4.4.

Correlations among Urban Design Qualities for 588 Block Faces in New York City

	Imageability	Enclosure	Human Scale	Transparency	Complexity
Imageability	1.0000				
Enclosure	0.0917	1.0000			
Human scale	0.3594	0.2986	1.0000		
Transparency	0.3483	0.5278	0.2951	1.0000	
Complexity	0.7480	0.1438	0.4171	0.2814	1.0000

enclosure) to 0.748 (imageability and complexity). To some extent, these correlations are an artifact of measure construction, because some indicators are included in multiple design constructs. For instance, the number of people and the presence of outdoor dining are indicators for both imageability and complexity. Enclosure, human scale, and transparency also share indicators with one another.

Urban design qualities varied across the city. Table 4.5 shows mean scores by borough. Mean scores for imageability were highest in Manhattan and Brooklyn; blocks in the Bronx had the lowest imageability. Enclosure was highest in Manhattan, followed by the Bronx; Queens and Staten Island had the lowest average enclosure. On human scale, interestingly, Queens and Staten Island scored almost as well as Manhattan, while the Bronx and Brooklyn had lower average scores. Manhattan had relatively high average scores on transparency, while Staten Island scored the lowest. Borough averages for complexity were fairly similar, with Brooklyn scoring the highest and the Bronx the lowest. Table 4.5 also displays descriptive information for the neighborhood (tract-level) characteristics of the block faces included in the study. (Block faces located in tracts with no resident population are excluded from this part of the table and from the analyses reported below.)

Tables 4.6 and 4.7 display the results of the regression analyses. Table 4.6 includes two models. The first uses a single measure of neighborhood age: the proportion of housing units built after 1939. The second model substitutes the more detailed measures for age of housing. The models also include measures of urban form and income and adjust for borough location. Associations with neighborhood age varied across the urban design indicators. The proportion of housing built after 1939 was significantly and negatively associated with enclosure, human scale, and transparency but not with imageability or

Table 4.5.
Urban Design Qualities and Tract-Level Neighborhood Characteristics of Measured Block Faces

	Bronx	Brooklyn	Manhattan	Queens	Staten Island
Urban design qualities					
Number of block faces	101	173	78	186	50
Imageability	3.36	3.74	3.87	3.45	3.43
Enclosure	3.20	3.11	3.43	2.83	2.91
Human scale	2.80	2.83	3.08	3.00	3.04
Transparency	2.71	2.77	3.11	2.50	2.11
Complexity	4.52	5.01	4.86	4.77	4.77
Tract-level characteristics					
Number of blocks	100	170	77	185	50
% of housing built:					
1940 and later	70.1	53.9	53.0	72.0	76.7
1940–1949	16.7	15.9	12.0	19.0	7.3
1950–1959	18.3	13.6	9.8	23.3	14.5
1960–1969	15.5	11.9	10.6	17.0	18.9
1970 and later	19.6	12.6	20.5	12.8	36.1
Population density	22,531	19,125	33,286	11,996	6,207
% of floor area commercial	11.3	18.8	39.3	15.4	5.7
Median household income	29,913	36,186	66,105	50,228	54,510

complexity. In the second set of analyses, neighborhoods with a larger proportion of housing built during the 1960s had higher imageability scores. For the other four urban design qualities, blocks located in neighborhoods with more recently built housing tended to have lower scores, although the coefficient and significance levels varied. Population density was positively associated with imageability, enclosure, transparency, and complexity but had no significant association with human scale. The proportion of commercial floor area was significantly and positively associated with transparency but not with any other urban design qualities. Last, median household income was significantly and positively associated with human scale but not with the other urban design qualities.

We also examined whether these neighborhood characteristics can account for the differences in urban design across New York City's five boroughs. Table 4.7 presents results for two models. Model 1 includes only dummy variables

Table 4.6.
OLS Regression Coefficients from Analyses Predicting Urban Design Qualities

	Imageability		Enclosure		Human Scale		Transparency		Complexity	
	Model 1	Model 2	Model 1	Model 2	Model 1	Model 2	Model 1	Model 2	Model 1	Model 2
Housing 1940–2000	−0.0345		−1.059‡		−0.493†		−0.513‡		−0.413	
	(0.221)		(0.160)		(0.179)		(0.107)		(0.238)	
Housing 1940–1949		0.959		−1.651‡		−1.417‡		−0.713†		−0.377
		(0.522)		(0.378)		(0.424)		(0.254)		(0.561)
Housing 1950–1959		−0.852		−0.442		−0.0917		−0.229		−0.927*
		(0.439)		(0.318)		(0.356)		(0.214)		(0.472)
Housing 1960–1969		0.804*		−1.606‡		−0.499		−0.815‡		0.551
		(0.398)		(0.288)		(0.323)		(0.194)		(0.428)
Housing 1970–2000		−0.250		−0.963‡		−0.690†		−0.432†		−0.874†
		(0.302)		(0.218)		(0.245)		(0.147)		(0.324)
Natural log of population density	0.281‡	0.276‡	0.167‡	0.172‡	0.0614	0.0757	0.260‡	0.261‡	0.242‡	0.251‡
	(0.0543)	(0.0550)	(0.0392)	(0.0398)	(0.0439)	(0.0446)	(0.0263)	(0.0268)	(0.0582)	(0.0591)
% commercial	0.00105	0.00149	0.00241	0.00224	−0.00256	−0.00253	0.00564‡	0.00554‡	0.00321	0.00370
	(0.00239)	(0.00240)	(0.00173)	(0.00174)	(0.00194)	(0.00195)	(0.00116)	(0.00117)	(0.00257)	(0.00258)
Median income	0.00150	0.00209	0.00252	0.00210	0.00659‡	0.00624‡	0.000195	0.000112	0.00158	0.00187
	(0.00226)	(0.00226)	(0.00163)	(0.00164)	(0.00183)	(0.00183)	(0.00110)	(0.00110)	(0.00243)	(0.00243)
Constant	0.842	0.737	1.906‡	1.926‡	2.388‡	2.501‡	0.568	0.422	2.475‡	2.378†
	(0.608)	(0.620)	(0.439)	(0.449)	(0.564)	(0.504)	(0.338)	(0.302)	(0.748)	(0.753)
R-squared	0.101	0.115	0.174	0.184	0.058	0.069	0.361	0.366	0.065	0.078

Note: Standard errors are in parentheses. Boldface font indicates that the coefficient is statistically significant at the p < 0.05 level. The number of observations in all models is 582. All models include indicators for borough location.

* p < .05, † p < .01, ‡ p < .001.

Table 4.7.

Associations between New York City Boroughs and Urban Design Qualities Before (Model 1) and After (Model 2) Adjustment for Neighborhood Age, Population Density, Commercial Land Use, and Median Income

	Imageability		Enclosure		Human Scale		Transparency		Complexity	
	Model 1	Model 2	Model 1	Model 2	Model 1	Model 2	Model 1	Model 2	Model 1	Model 2
Bronx	**-0.510**‡	-0.322	-0.213	0.162	**-0.269***	0.00143	**-0.402**‡	-0.0792	**-0.354***	-0.0451
	(0.150)	(0.190)	(0.111)	(0.138)	(0.119)	(0.154)	(0.0785)	(0.0927)	(0.158)	(0.205)
Brooklyn	-0.111	0.0515	**-0.298**†	-0.102	**-0.233***	-0.0606	**-0.335**‡	-0.111	0.134	0.333
	(0.135)	(0.166)	(0.100)	(0.120)	(0.108)	(0.134)	(0.0711)	(0.0808)	(0.143)	(0.178)
Queens	**-0.419**†	-0.143	**-0.595**‡	-0.162	-0.0720	0.117	**-0.610**‡	-0.161	-0.107	0.269
	(0.134)	(0.172)	(0.0989)	(0.124)	(0.107)	(0.136)	(0.0702)	(0.0838)	(0.142)	(0.185)
Staten Island	**-0.450***	0.0468	**-0.508**‡	0.0435	-0.0296	0.159	**-1.003**‡	**-0.360**†	-0.113	0.482
	(0.179)	(0.229)	(0.132)	(0.166)	(0.143)	(0.183)	(0.0940)	(0.111)	(0.190)	(0.246)
Constant	**3.880**‡	0.880	**3.418**‡	**2.088**‡	**3.073**‡	**2.388**‡	**3.113**‡	0.583	**4.887**†	**2.378**†
	(0.112)	(0.700)	(0.0831)	(0.507)	(0.0898)	(0.564)	(0.0590)	(0.341)	(0.119)	(0.753)
R-squared	0.036	0.115	0.073	0.184	0.017	0.058	0.198	0.366	0.025	0.078

Note: Standard errors are in parentheses. Boldface font indicates that the coefficient is statistically significant at the p < 0.05 level. The number of observations in all models is 582. Model 1 includes indicators for borough location (with Manhattan as the omitted category). Model 2 includes indicators for borough location as well as all neighborhood characteristics shown in model 2 of table 4.6

* p < .05, † p < .01, ‡ p < .001.

for the boroughs, with Manhattan as the reference (omitted) category. Model 2 adjusts for neighborhood age, urban form, and income (results are from the model 2 in table 4.6). Table 4.7 compares borough indicators from these two models. In Model 1, there are significant differences across boroughs in urban design characteristics. Compared with the blocks observed in Manhattan, blocks observed in the Bronx, Queens, and Staten Island had lower imageability; Brooklyn, Queens, and Staten Island had lower levels of enclosure; the Bronx and Brooklyn scored lower on human scale; all four other boroughs scored lower than Manhattan on transparency; and the Bronx had lower complexity. In model 2, which controls statistically for neighborhood characteristics, all but one of these cross-borough differences became insignificant. In the one exception, transparency was lower in Staten Island than in Manhattan even after adjusting for neighborhood characteristics. Based on these analyses, borough differences in urban design appear to be largely a function of differences in neighborhood age, urban form, and income.

Although the block face urban design measures do vary systematically across neighborhoods, it is worth noting that most of the variation in urban design remains unexplained after controlling for neighborhood age, urban form, income, and borough. These neighborhood characteristics explain more than a third of the variation in transparency but only 7 to 8 percent of the variation in human scale and complexity. Put another way, although areas with higher density and mixed land use tended to have higher urban design scores, population density and land use mix would be inadequate proxies for block face–level urban design. As our data suggest, the visual and social character of the street-level environment varies in ways that are not fully captured by simple measures of urban form.

New Strategies for Measuring Urban Design

Ultimately, our intent is to develop measurement strategies that are scalable—that can be implemented in large-scale studies relating the built environment to social, psychological, and health outcomes. Although in-person audits are well suited to measuring the streetscape as pedestrians experience it, the time required for the audit itself and for travel to and from the neighborhood makes this kind of data collection infeasible for studies with a large or geographically dispersed study area. Moreover, in-person audits are sometimes perceived as intrusive by neighborhood residents and can involve risk to research personnel (Caughy, O'Campo, and Patterson 2001).

For this reason, researchers are exploring alternative means of collecting objective measures of urban design. In one such effort, supported by the same RWJF Active Living Research grant that funded our in-person audit in New York City, we employed data from the US Census, the New York City government, and other public, nonprofit, and proprietary sources to develop "digital" equivalents of items in the MIUDQ protocol (Purciel et al. 2009). For instance, to identify blocks with outdoor dining, we obtained permit data from the New York City Department of Consumer Affairs, which licenses outdoor eateries. To measure the proportion of historic building frontage, we used the PLUTO tax lot data, which include information on year of building construction. Noise level was proxied using estimates of traffic volume for different classes of roads. After developing these digital measures, we combined them to create digital versions of the urban design scale scores. We were unable to identify digital equivalents for eight of the individual items, including street furniture, building colors, and public art. Because not all individual items were available in digital form, we adjusted the weights used to construct the urban design scores; the revised weights were based on coefficients from reanalyses of the original data that excluded the items for which we had no digital equivalents.

We assessed the validity of the digital measures by comparing them with the in-person audit measures for the 588 blocks (Purciel et al. 2009). The validity of the individual digital items varied substantially: correlations between field and digital measures ranged from 0.16 for long sight lines to 0.95 for number of buildings. Correlations between the observed and digital urban design scores were high for imageability (0.72), transparency (0.71), and complexity (0.89); moderate for enclosure (0.53); and low for human scale (0.28). As noted, some of the items for human scale were unavailable in digital form. In addition, human scale includes one item—long sight lines—for which the digital measure was relatively poor (correlation of 0.16).

This study can be taken as a proof of concept for the development of digital measures based on in-person audit protocols. Although our work was limited by the lack of high-quality digital equivalents for some items in the MIUDQ protocol, in principle this approach is feasible now in some locales and will become increasingly viable over time. As municipalities and nonprofit or private organizations collect a wider array of spatially referenced data about the urban environment, researchers will be able to construct digital measures of urban design with higher validity and precision.

In addition, we and other researchers are exploring the use of tools such as Google Street View to measure features of the neighborhood environment (Badland et al. 2010; Clarke et al. 2010; Rundle et al. 2011; Odgers et al. 2012; Wilson et al. 2012). This approach has important advantages compared with both in-person audits and use of GIS data. First, although the images must still be manually coded, as with in-person audits, researchers need not travel to the study site. Second, Google Street View images are available for most urban areas in the United States and for some rural areas as well, allowing researchers to use measures that are comparable across place. By contrast, GIS data are compiled by municipal governments or planning agencies and the measures available can differ substantially across jurisdiction. Neighborhood measurement using Google Street View has some disadvantages: some items cannot be measured at all (noise, odors), and others have low reliability because they are small or temporally variable (Rundle et al. 2011). In many instances, however, Street View or other omnidirectional imagery offers opportunities for neighborhood assessment that would otherwise be infeasible.

With funding from the National Institutes of Health, the Built Environment and Health group at Columbia University is currently developing protocols for using Google Street View to measure neighborhood environments (Rundle et al. 2011). The measures being implemented in Street View include items from MIUDQ as well as the Minnesota-Irvine Inventory (Boarnet et al. 2006), the Pedestrian Environment Data Scan (Clifton, Livi-Smith, and Rodriguez 2007), the Project for Human Development in Chicago Neighborhoods, and the New York City Housing and Vacancy Survey. We are conducting reliability assessments in a national sample of neighborhoods and developing measures for use in analysis of the Fragile Families and Child Wellbeing Study, a panel study of families in twenty cities. In the course of this work, we have also developed a web application—the "Computer assisted neighborhood visual assessment system" (CANVAS)—for running virtual neighborhood audit studies. CANVAS includes a study administrator interface, an analytics subsystem, and a user interface that allows coders to view blocks via Street View on one screen and to input the corresponding data on the other.

As these ongoing efforts suggest, unconventional data sources such as Google Street View offer novel opportunities for assessment of urban design. Theoretically grounded tools such as the MIUDQ can be implemented in multiple ways, with the choice of measurement method dependent on the available data and the size and geographic extent of the study area. While in-person assessment is likely to remain the gold standard, the value of audit protocols such as the MIUDQ can be extended by implementation in other formats. Although use of Street View may afford lower reliability or validity than in-person audits of individual blocks, its efficiency allows researchers to audit a larger sample of blocks, thus the validity of neighborhood measurement is expected to be higher.

Conclusions

This chapter describes the implementation of the MIUDQ protocol in a sample of New York City neighborhoods that vary in terms of both density and land use mix. Our study shows that the MIUDQ protocol, which was initially developed primarily in downtown or mixed-use areas, can be used across a wide range of urban environments, including areas that are suburban in character as well as the most densely settled neighborhoods in the United States.

We also found that urban design qualities are associated with—although far from determined by—neighborhood age, urban form, and income. Imageability was higher among blocks located in high-density neighborhoods and also (unexpectedly) in neighborhoods with a higher fraction of housing built in the 1960s. Enclosure was higher in neighborhoods that were older and higher density. Human scale was higher in neighborhoods that were older and more affluent. Transparency was higher in older neighborhoods and in those with higher density and more commercial land use. Complexity was higher in higher-density neighborhoods and in those with less housing built in the 1950s or after 1969. These relationships, which are largely consistent with theoretical expectations, increase confidence in the validity of the MIUDQ urban design measures.

Next steps for research include replication in other locales; comparison with results from New York City would be informative and would extend our understanding of how urban design qualities vary across context. Continued work to implement the MIUDQ using alternative data sources such as GIS data and Google Street View would allow measurement of larger or more geographically dispersed areas, supporting cross-place comparison of urban design as well as study of how urban design shapes human behaviors, health, and well-being.

Standardized measures of urban design are an important resource for the study of human responses to urban design qualities, including preferences as well as such behaviors as walking or social interaction. Research validating the MIUDQ that describes how urban design measures are associated with physical activity or social cohesion is a logical extension of this work. Such studies would support further development of the MIUDQ protocol itself. For instance, there may be thresholds beyond which more of an attribute adds little to or even detracts from the pleasurable experience of a place. For example, pedestrian traffic (a component of imageability and complexity) may be stimulating in moderation but irritating or even intimidating in excess. It would also be helpful to know how human response to urban design is affected by other qualities not currently measured in the MIUDQ, such as natural elements (street trees) or physical disorder.

CHAPTER FIVE

Validation of Measures

This chapter builds on earlier chapters to, for the first time, validate urban design measures against pedestrian counts on 588 street segments in New York City. This is the logical next step using the field measurements and pedestrian counts described in chapter 4. An effort is made to distinguish which measures, if any, influence levels of pedestrian activity after controlling for surrounding density, land use diversity, and other so-called D variables that have been found to influence travel behavior.

The study in this chapter breaks new ground in three respects. It is the first to validate micro-urban design measures against pedestrian counts. It is the first planning research study to use web-based street imagery from Google Street View, Bing StreetSide, and EveryScape to establish the reliability of manual pedestrian counts conducted in the field. It also is the first to use Walk Scores to measure a key D measure, destination accessibility.

Data

Primary data for this study was compiled by the Columbia University team, as described in chapter 4. For each block face in the sample, field observers measured all variables that compose the five urban design measures. They also counted pedestrians.

In an effort to make the process replicable, secondary data were limited to those that are publicly available in other parts of the country (see table 5.1). GIS data for the study area were acquired directly from the New York City Department of City Planning, including DCPLION street segment centerlines and MapPluto™ parcel layers. Census 2010 SF1 100% and TIGER 2010 census block shapefiles were used to calculate roadway network, land use, and demographic variables.

Table 5.1.
Secondary Data Sources

Data Type	Description	Source
Parcel data	Tax lot geodatabase with use and floor area attributes	City of New York, Department of City Planning
Road centerlines	Street centerline and classification	City of New York, Department of City Planning
Transit stops	Subway entrance and exit points	MTA New York City Transit
2010 census block	2010 SF1 population and households shapefile	ESRI, US Census

Measures

The measures used in this validation exercise represent a "gold standard" for such studies, carefully measured in the field or calculated using high-quality GIS data. In the case of the dependent variable—pedestrian activity—field counts were also checked for reliability. We believe it is possible to construct such measures, and replicate results, in many other urban areas around the country.

Pedestrian Activity

The dependent variable explained in this study is the average number of people encountered on four passes up and down a given block face. As described in chapter 4, Columbia University observers visited each of the 588 street segments and conducted four field counts of the number of pedestrians along the block face at a particular time. The students walked the length of the segment one time for each count and included every pedestrian they encountered during that exercise, noting the time of day and weather conditions observed for that period.

Because the sample size is small for these counts (n = 4) and the counts are not independent but, rather, made in succession at different times and different days of the week for different street segments, we needed to establish the reliability of our dependent variable. This was done by counting pedestrians on three websites that provide street-level imagery and comparing these counts to the manual counts. The three sites are Google Street View, Bing StreetSide, and EveryScape. The same street was filmed at different times by the different suppliers of imagery. Thus we, with the average field counts, have four independent counts of pedestrian activity.

Google Street View is a technology available over the Internet through Google Maps and Google Earth software, which allows users to see panoramic street-level imagery from points along public streets and highways. The imagery is collected through the use of a vehicle specially retrofitted with overhead photographic equipment that captures panoramic views for the period in which the vehicle traveled through. Launched in 2007 with limited imagery available for only a handful of US cities, Street View has proven enormously popular and has since expanded to include imagery from thousands of towns and cities with at least partial coverage currently available across all six continents with road networks. The technology allows users to view specific areas of real estate and points of interest and to virtually wander through the street-level environment as though they themselves were driving through it.

Owing to its relative newness, Google Street View has rarely been utilized in published research. Initial research in the planning field has largely focused on the viability of Street View as a cost-effective alternative to conducting physical neighborhood and streetscape audits, chiefly in measuring the walkability and bikeability of individual areas. To our knowledge, that body of research is limited to five studies, all published since 2010 (Clarke et al. 2010; Badland et al. 2010; Odgers et al. 2012; Rundle et al. 2011; Wilson et al. 2012). Three of those studies had small sample sizes—38 street segments in New York City (Rundle et al. 2011), 48 street segments in Auckland, New Zealand (Badland et al. 2010), and 60 blocks in Chicago (Clarke et al. 2010). Additionally, the Chicago study was handicapped in that field audits were conducted five years before virtual audits were undertaken. Only the Wilson et al. and Odgers et al. studies had large samples—375 street segments across Indianapolis and St. Louis and 1,102 neighborhoods across Great Britain, respectively. The Wilson et al. study is also notable in that it measured the reliability of video street level imagery obtained commercially (including archived imagery and imagery generated concurrently with field audits) in addition to Google Street View imagery.

All of the studies found that Google Street View offers a reliable alternative to neighborhood audits conducted in the field. "Overall, Google Street View provided a resource-efficient and reliable alternative to physically auditing the attributes of neighborhood streetscapes associated with walking and cycling"

(Badland et al. 2010). However, both Clarke et al. (2010) and Rundle et al. (2011) caution against using Street View to make "finely grained observations" (Clarke et al. 2010, p. 1224), including those related to graffiti or the presence of litter, finding that they exhibited lower scores of reliability.

As we were attempting to verify the reliability of manual pedestrian counts, it was important to have more than one virtual count. Microsoft's StreetSide service, available through its Bing Maps platform, provides street-level imagery in a user environment very similar to Google Street View. Launched in 2009, StreetSide imagery is generally available at a resolution very comparable to most imagery provided by Google Street View. It is only operable in significant urban centers in the United States and Canada and is much less expansive in its coverage area than Google Street View. Within New York City, StreetSide is operable widely in Manhattan and Brooklyn, with more limited coverage in the boroughs of the Bronx and Queens. There is currently no StreetSide imagery available for Staten Island.

EveryScape is an online mapping service that also allows users to access street-level panoramic imagery in a format very similar to Google's Street View platform. Launched in 2007, EveryScape is unique in that it allows users to virtually enter the interiors of particular stores and restaurants (businesses that partner with and compensate EveryScape for the service). The imagery provided by EveryScape is presented at a slightly lower resolution than Google Street View but certainly at a sufficient quality to identify pedestrians. EveryScape is also far more limited in its coverage than Street View; the platform currently features street-level imagery for only forty-seven cities, forty-four of which are located in the United States. Within New York City, EveryScape offers street-level imagery only for the boroughs of Brooklyn and Manhattan, with no coverage of the Bronx, Queens, or Staten Island.

We performed two tests of reliability with respect to pedestrian counts. The first was a test of inter-rater reliability for the counts from the different websites. It would seem a simple matter to count pedestrians using static images, but because pedestrians are partially hidden by other pedestrians, cars, and trees, images (particularly EveryScape) are sometimes blurry, and observers suffer from fatigue, there is some error associated with counts for the same streets from the same websites. One student observer counted pedestrians on all streets for which imagery was available. Three others independently counted pedestrians for a random subsample of thirty block faces from the larger sample. The sample of segments included high pedestrian counts and low pedestrian counts.

Various statistical techniques may be used to assess inter-rater reliability in studies like this, where multiple individuals independently analyze the same set of cases. As in chapters 3 and 4, we used intra-class correlation coefficients (ICCs), representing the ratio of between-group variance to total variance of counts (Fleiss 1981).

Our sample size of thirty was comparable to similar studies conducted by Pikora et al. (2002) and Clifton, Livi-Smith, and Rodriguez (2007). Inter-rater reliability was high, particularly for Google and Bing (see table 5.2). As a general guide, we followed the adjectival ratings suggested by Landis and Koch (1977), who considered Kappa scores between 0.8 and 1.0 as indicating almost perfect agreement and those between 0.6 and 0.8 as indicating sub-stantial agreement. Inter-rater agreement was almost perfect for Google and Bing and was substantial for EveryScape.

Table 5.2.
Intraclass Correlation Coefficients for a Sample of Thirty Counts by Four Observers

	Intraclass Correlation Coefficients (ICCs)	Level of Agreement (Landis and Koch 1977)
Google	0.960	Perfect
Bing	0.979	Perfect
EveryScape	0.796	Substantial

The other test of reliability was to compare field counts conducted by ob-servers from Columbia University to counts from web-based street imagery. Ideally, the Columbia team would have conducted field counts for extended and standard periods at each block face. Vehicle traffic counts are done in this manner. However, vehicle counts are usually automated rather than manual, and when they are manual (as at individual intersections), sample sizes are small. The number of block faces in this study precluded such a labor-inten-sive approach. Instead, we were forced to rely on four consecutive counts, in a random period, for each block face. This raises issues of reliability.

To test whether the field counts, in fact, are reliable indicators of pedestrian activity, we conducted a test of equivalence reliability. Equivalence reliability is the extent to which different variables measure the same underlying construct—in this case, pedestrian activity. Equivalence reliability is determined by relating values of the different variables to one another to highlight the degree of relationship or association.

We had already established that web-based pedestrian counts by different raters are reliable. We next compared counts by one rater for each website to field counts. Sample sizes are different because only Google Street View has imagery for all 588 block faces. Equivalence reliability is judged with Cronbach's alpha (table 5.3). Cronbach's alpha is widely used in the social sciences to see if items—questions, raters, indicators—measure the same thing. If independent counts—four based on fieldwork and three based on street imagery—agree, we can assume that the field counts are reliable measures of pedestrian activity. Some professionals require a reliability of 0.70 or higher before they will use an instrument. In the case of psychometric tests, most fall within the range of 0.75 to 0.83. Our alpha values are consistent with these guidelines for two out of three websites.

Table 5.3.
Cronbach's Alpha Values for Field Counts versus Web Counts by One Rater

	Field Counts vs. Google Counts	Field Counts vs. Bing Counts	Field Counts vs. EveryScape Counts
Cronbach's alpha	0.864	0.470	0.784
Sample size of block face	588	169	201

D Variables

The explanatory variables of primary interest are the five urban design measures—imageability, enclosure, human scale, transparency, and complexity. These were computed for each block face in the sample by substituting field measurements by the Columbia University team into equations in table 5.4 with the following modification. The equations for imageability and complexity include the variable "number of people" encountered while walking the segment. This is also the dependent variable we are attempting to model. We could not very well use pedestrian counts to explain pedestrian counts. Hence, the calculation of these two urban design measures excluded the pedestrian count term.

For control variables, we drew on characterizations of the D variables from

Table 5.4.

Summary of Models

Design Quality	Significant Physical Features	Coefficient	p-value
Imageability	People (#)	0.0239	‹ 0.001
	Proportion of historic buildings	0.970	‹ 0.001
	Courtyards/plazas/parks (#)	0.414	‹ 0.001
	Outdoor dining (y/n)	0.644	‹ 0.001
	Buildings with nonrectangular silhouettes (#)	0.0795	0.036
	Noise level (rating)	−0.183	0.045
	Major landscape features (#)	0.722	0.049
	Buildings with identifiers (#)	0.111	0.083
Enclosure	Proportion of street wall—same side	0.716	0.001
	Proportion of street wall—opposite side	0.940	0.002
	Proportion of sky across	−2.193	0.021
	Long sight lines (#)	−0.308	0.035
	Proportion of sky ahead	−1.418	0.055
Human scale	Long sight lines (#)	−0.744	‹ 0.001
	All street furniture and other street items (#)	0.0364	‹ 0.001
	Proportion of first floor with windows	1.099	‹ 0.001
	Building height—same side	−0.00304	0.033
	Small planters (#)	0.0496	0.047
	Urban designer (y/n)	0.382	0.066
Transparency	Proportion of first floor with windows	1.219	0.002
	Proportion of active uses	0.533	0.004
	Proportion of street wall—same side	0.666	0.011
Complexity	People (#)	0.0268	‹ 0.001
	Buildings (#)	0.0510	0.008
	Dominant building colors (#)	0.177	0.031
	Accent colors (#)	0.108	0.043
	Outdoor dining (y/n)	0.367	0.045
	Public art (#)	0.272	0.066

Note: Models of imageability, human scale, and complexity were reestimated since the publication of the project's final report (Ewing et al. 2005), which accounts for the minor differences in variables and coefficient values.

Ewing and Cervero (2010) and Ewing et al. (2011). The D variables are density, diversity, design, destination accessibility, distance to transit, and demographics. They have been used in literally hundreds of studies to explain travel behavior. Density is always measured as a variable of interest per unit of area. Two density measures were computed for the quarter-mile buffer around each street segment. One is the average floor area ratio, computed as the total building floor area for all parcels within the buffer, divided by the total area of tax lots (buffer *FAR*). The other is the average population density, computed as the population of all census blocks whose centroids fell within the buffer divided by the total area of residential tax lots whose centroids fell within the buffer, measured in one thousand residents per square mile (*population density*).

Diversity is related to the number of different land uses in a given area and the degree to which they are balanced in land area, floor area, or employment. An entropy measure of diversity was computed with the formula

entropy = –[residential share*LN (residential share) + retail share*LN (retail share) + office share*LN (office share)]/ LN (3)

where the shares were computed based on floor area of each use for tax lots within the buffer.

While much of the focus here is on subtler measures of urban design, gross metrics of design were computed with GIS. One was intersection density, computed as the number of intersections within the quarter-mile buffer around each street segment divided by the gross area of the buffer in square miles (*intersection density*). The other was the proportion of four-way intersections within the buffer (*proportion 4-way*).

The D variable destination accessibility was represented by Walk Scores (*walk score*). Walk Score is an Internet-based platform that rates the walkability of a specific address on a numeric scale (from 0 to 100) by compiling the number of nearby stores and amenities within a one-mile radius of a location. The platform specifically measures walkability relative to thirteen amenity categories: grocery stores, coffee shops, restaurants, bars, movie theaters, schools, parks, libraries, bookstores, fitness centers, drug stores, hardware stores, and clothing/music stores (Carr et al. 2011). Amenities within a quarter mile receive maximum points, and no points are awarded for amenities farther than one mile. For this study, an address at the approximate midpoint of each block face was retrieved using Google Street View and then entered into the Walk Score website to obtain a score for each segment.

The authors identified two studies that tested the reliability of Walk Scores in measuring neighborhood walkability and access to amenities (Carr et al. 2011; Duncan et al. 2011). Both studies used GIS measures to validate Walk Score data; Carr et al. (2011) for 379 addresses in Providence, Rhode Island, and Duncan et al. (2011) for 754 addresses in four US metropolitan areas in distinct geographical regions. Both studies concluded that Walk Score represented a valid and reliable measure of access to walkable amenities. Duncan et al. (2011, p. 4161) added that the platform's reliability held up "in multiple geographic locations and at multiple spatial scales."

Using ArcInfo Network Analyst (ESRI 2009) and the New York City road centerline shapefile, a network analysis was performed to find the shortest distance from each study segment center point to the closest rail station. The result was a mile distance-to-transit variable related to each study segment (*distance to rail*).

The only demographic variable computed was average household size for blocks whose centroids fell with the quarter-mile buffer around each block face (*household size*). We could have estimated median household income or per capita income from the 2006–2010 American Community Survey, but data were only available at the large geography of the census tract.

Reasoning that pedestrian counts on a given block face depend as much on land uses along the block face as on development patterns within easy walking distance, we estimated three additional D variables: average floor area ratio for the block face, computed as the total building floor area for parcels abutting the street, divided by the total area of tax lots (*block FAR*); an entropy measure based on floor area for parcels abutting the street, computed with the formula above (*block entropy*); and proportion of retail frontage along the block face, on the assumption that retail frontage generates more pedestrian activity than other frontage (*proportion retail*).

One final control variable used in this study is the length of each block face (*block length*). The simple theory is that after controlling for other influences, the longer the block, the more pedestrians will occupy it at any given time.

Analysis

Our method of analysis was dictated by the distribution of the dependent variable, the average pedestrian count for four passes up and down each block face rounded to the nearest integer. Many streets have low pedestrian counts, few streets have high pedestrian counts, and no streets can have negative counts (see figure 5.1). Counts range from 0 to 176, with a mean value of 5.78 and a standard deviation of 12.97. The assumptions of ordinary least squares (OLS) regression are violated in this case. Specifically, the dependent variable is not normally distributed, and the error term will not be homoscedastic or normally distributed.

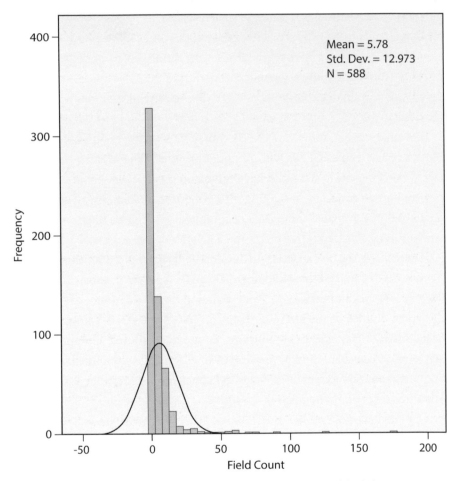

Figure 5.1. Frequency distribution of pedestrian counts for 588 block faces.

Two basic methods of analysis are available when the dependent variable is a count, with nonnegative integer values, many small values, and few large ones. The methods are Poisson regression and negative binomial regression, both fairly new to the planning field. They mostly have been used in crash studies because of the high skewed nature of crash counts (for example, Dumbaugh and Rae 2009; Marshall and Garrick 2011).

The models differ in their assumptions about the distribution of the dependent variable. Poisson regression is the appropriate model form if the mean and the variance of the dependent variable are equal. Negative binomial regression is appropriate if the dependent variable is overdispersed, meaning that the variance of counts is greater than the mean. Because the negative binomial distribution contains an extra parameter, it is a robust alternative to the Poisson model.

> A central distributional assumption of the Poisson model is the equivalence of the Poisson mean and variance. This assumption is rarely met with real data. Usually the variance exceeds the mean, resulting in what is termed *overdispersion*. . . . Overdispersion is, in fact, the norm and gives rise to a variety of other models that are extensions of the basic Poisson model. Negative binomial regression is nearly always thought of as the model to be used instead of Poisson when overdispersion is present in the data. (Hilbe 2011, p. 140)

Popular indicators of overdispersion are the Pearson and chi-square statistics divided by the degrees of freedom, so-called dispersion statistics. If these statistics are greater than 1.0, a model is said to be overdispersed (Hilbe 2011, pp. 88, 142). By these measures, we have overdispersion and the negative binomial model is more appropriate than the Poisson model. The Wald and likelihood ratio tests are also used to check for overdispersion (Greene 2012, p. 810). For our data, both tests reject the Poisson hypothesis of equidispersion. The likelihood ratio chi-square statistics for the tests against the null Poisson model exceed 1,000 for both models specified below. Alpha statistics (square root of Wald statistics) for the overdispersion parameters appear in table 5.5; both exceed 1.96, the critical value for significance.

Results

We used the econometric software package NLOGIT to estimate two negative binomial models of pedestrian counts (see table 5.5). Model 1 contains the standard D variables without the urban design measures, while model 2 includes the urban design measures.[1] Both models have highly significant likelihood ratio statistics (564.8 and 611.8), indicating a good fit to the data relative to a null model with only intercept terms. The likelihood ratio statistic of model 2 relative to model 1, 47.0 with 5 degrees of freedom, indicates that the fit is significantly better for model 2 at the 0.001 probability level.

In both models, the three density measures—buffer FAR, buffer population density, and block FAR—are directly and significantly related to pedestrian counts. One of two measures of street network design—proportion of four-way intersections—approaches significance and has the expected positive relationship to pedestrian counts, while the other—intersection density—is not significant. This is surprising, as intersection density is strongly associated with walking in household-level travel studies (Ewing and Cervero 2010). Our measures of buffer land use diversity—entropy—and destination accessibility—Walk Score—are not significant in either model. This is also surprising, given the emphasis on diversity and destination accessibility in the household travel literature (Ewing and Cervero 2010). Distance to rail is significant with the expected negative sign: pedestrian counts dropping off with distance. Block entropy approaches significance with the expected positive sign, while the proportion of retail frontage is highly significant. Apparently, having equal proportions of residential, retail, and office on a block face is less conducive to pedestrian activity than having a disproportionate share of retail frontage. Household size and block length are directly related to pedestrian counts at significant levels.

As for the urban design measures in model 2, one measure—transparency—stands out. Not only is transparency significant after controlling for other D variables, but it has greater significance than any of the standard D variables. This is a novel finding, to our knowledge the first time anything like this has been reported in the literature.

The fact the transparency is significant after controlling for retail frontage (though it attenuates the effect of retail frontage in the simple model) indicates that transparency is not a simple proxy for retail uses, whose storefronts often

---

[1] While multicollinearity would appear to be an issue with so many variables, it actually is not. The lowest tolerance value, that of buffer FAR, is 0.27 in model 2. Tolerance values are greater than 0.5 for ten of the variables in model 2.

have high transparency with display windows. Transparency, as we measured it, incorporates much more.

Among the other urban design variables, only human scale is positively related to pedestrian counts, and then only at the 0.10 significance level (table 5.5). Imageability and complexity, as we measured them, have no relationship to pedestrian activity. Enclosure is significant at the 0.10 level with an unexpected, negative sign. Perhaps the canyon-like streetscapes of the some New York streets detract from the walking experience.

Table 5.5.

Negative Binomial Regression Models of Pedestrian Counts (588 Block Faces)

	Model 1				Model 2			
	coeff.	std. error	t-ratio	p-value	coeff.	std. error	t-ratio	p-value
Intercept	−1.889	0.554	−3.41	‹ 0.001	−2.636	0.527	−5.00	‹ 0.001
FAR	0.153	0.024	6.42	‹ 0.001	0.130	0.024	5.45	‹ 0.001
Population density	0.008	0.024	4.14	‹ 0.001	0.008	0.002	3.99	‹ 0.001
Entropy	0.324	0.248	1.31	0.36	0.361	0.251	1.44	0.15
Intersection density	−0.0005	0.0008	−0.63	0.53	−0.0007	0.0008	−0.89	0.37
Proportion 4-way	0.435	0.247	1.76	0.078	0.390	0.243	1.60	0.11
Walk score	0.007	0.005	1.25	0.21	0.004	0.004	0.98	0.33
Distance to rail	−0.219	0.047	−4.66	‹ 0.001	−0.206	0.048	−4.26	‹ 0.001
Block FAR	0.043	0.014	3.15	0.002	0.041	0.013	3.21	0.002
Block entropy	0.273	0.174	1.57	0.12	0.282	0.174	1.63	0.11
Proportion retail	1.148	0.137	8.39	‹ 0.001	0.642	0.146	4.39	‹ 0.001
Household size	0.286	0.082	3.48	‹ 0.001	0.254	0.087	2.93	0.004
Block length	6.481	1.056	6.14	‹ 0.001	7.202	1.242	5.80	‹ 0.001
Imageability					−0.062	0.060	−1.05	0.30
Enclosure					−0.112	0.065	−1.74	0.083
Human scale					0.129	0.067	1.93	0.053
Transparency					0.573	0.088	6.51	‹ 0.001
Complexity					−0.046	0.063	−0.73	0.47
N		588				588		
Alpha	0.520	0.051	10.26	‹ 0.001	0.447	0.047	9.44	‹ 0.001
Likelihood ratio statistic (df)		564.8 (12)				611.8 (17)		

Discussion

This chapter has sought to explain pedestrian counts on 588 block faces in New York City in terms of D variables—density, diversity, design, destination accessibility, distance to transit, and demographics. Most of the standard D variables tested have the expected relationships to pedestrian counts at high significant levels. Among the design variables used as predictors are measures developed by Ewing and Handy (2009) representing the urban design qualities of imageability, enclosure, human scale, transparency, and complexity. The urban design measures as a group add significantly to the explanatory power of our models, and one measure—transparency—proves more significant than any other variable in this multivariate analysis.

What are the implications for planning practice? First, context is important, particularly floor area ratio, population density, and land use mix within a quarter mile of sampled streets. Zoning can be amended to achieve high values of each of these variables. For street life, streets themselves should have high floor area ratios and predominantly retail frontage. They should also exhibit the urban design quality of transparency.

Transparency is the urban design quality most often defined and prescribed in urban design guidelines and land development codes. Some definitions of transparency are strictly qualitative, whereas others are quantitative. The concept is operationalized almost always in terms of windows as a percentage of ground floor facade. San Jose's operational definition is typical:

> Transparency: A street level development standard that defines a requirement for clear or lightly tinted glass in terms of a percentage of the façade area between an area falling within 2 feet and 20 feet above the adjacent sidewalk or walkway. (City of San Jose 2004)

However, the measure of transparency used in this study is broader. It incorporates three operational variables: the proportion of first-floor facade with windows; the proportion of active uses at street level; and the proportion of street wall along the frontage. Active uses are defined as shops, restaurants, public parks, and other uses that generate significant pedestrian traffic. Inactive uses include blank walls, driveways, parking lots, vacant lots, abandoned buildings, and offices with little or no pedestrian traffic. In regard to residential uses, when the density is more than ten units per acre, we assume that the land use is active. Street walls are defined as continuous walls or building facades adjacent to the sidewalk. Facades set back by parking or by lawn and driveways do not count as street walls. Intersecting streets and ends of blocks do not count against the proportion of street wall.

To achieve this broader definition of transparency, codes will need to be restructured in a more fundamental way. What comes to mind are the requirements and restrictions of form-based codes, many of which provide for windows, active uses, or street walls. One of the best known and most successful applications of form-based codes is in Arlington County, Virginia's Columbia Pike Special Revitalization District. The form-based code requires that buildings be built to a required building line adjacent to the property line and sidewalk (see figure 5.2). The street is thus a "coherent space, with consistent building forms on both sides of the street" (Arlington County 2003, p. 4.1). Generally, retail uses are required on the ground floor of main street sites. "Retail" is broadly defined to include comparison retail stores, convenience retail stores, personal business services, professional offices, restaurants, grocery stores, and hotel, theater, and other uses that "provide visual interest and create active street life" (p. 3.6). Main street building facades are required to

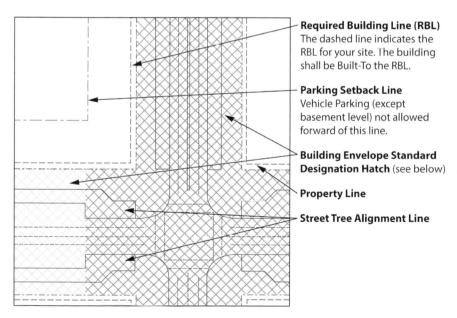

Figure 5.2. Columbia Pike Regulating Plan.

have 60 to 90 percent fenestration (measured as a percentage of the facade that is between 2 and 10 feet above the fronting sidewalk). Upper-story facades are required to have 30 to 70 percent fenestration (measured for each story as a percentage of the facade that is between 3 and 9 feet above the finished floor).

We conclude by acknowledging limitations of this study both in validity and reliability. Obviously, New York City is unique among cities in the United States, which limits the external validity of our findings. While wide swaths of the city, including much of Staten Island and the North Bronx, are suburban in nature, New York City is overwhelmingly urban. Four of five counties that comprise the city rank as the four most compact counties in the nation (Ewing, Schieber, and Zegeer 2003). The metropolitan area has by far the highest walk mode share of any large metropolitan area, 21.4 percent (Federal Highway Administration 2009). Our first research recommendation would be to repeat this validation study in more typical cities.

The main threat to the reliability of our results is the limited counts done on each block face. The day and time of the counts were variable. Only four counts were done on each block face, as field observers walked up and down the block. Our second research recommendation would be to conduct longer standardized counts on each street segment in any future study.

If replicated, we believe that this study and its progeny will provide urban planners and urban designers with some of the clearest and most compelling guidance yet available for creating vibrant street life.

CHAPTER SIX

Field Manual

The measures used in previous studies to characterize the built environment have been mostly general qualities, such as neighborhood density and street connectivity. What do these measures tell us about what it is like to walk down a street? The answer is not much, and that's why measuring urban design qualities is so important. In the previous chapters, we identified five urban design qualities that have a relationship with the overall walkability of a place:

- imageability
- enclosure
- human scale
- transparency
- complexity

In this chapter we present detailed procedures for measuring these qualities. We considered many other qualities referenced in the literature. We tried, unsuccessfully, to operationalize others. But, based on the work we've described in this book, the urban design qualities we've identified here appear to have significant relationships to walkability and great potential to be measured objectively and reliably.

Getting Started

Our statistical analyses demonstrated that simple measurements of physical features found in the environment can help explain urban design qualities (chapter 3). In addition, we found that urban design qualities can help explain the overall walkability of a place (chapter 3). It will come as no surprise then, that measuring urban design qualities will require a good amount of walking and observing. Our protocols will require you to count many different physical features. For instance, to measure imageability, our instructions prompt you to count small planters and also buildings with identifying signs. In most cases, you will find it easiest to walk your study area several times, counting or measuring each different feature prompted in our instructions on a different walk-through.

Be sure to wear comfortable shoes and find a day with good weather. You will probably spend much of your time outdoors. Since your measurements will be taken in the "real world," make sure that you are always aware of your surroundings as you count features and estimate other features. Bringing a partner can be helpful and is encouraged. One person could make the measurements while the other could hold materials and, most important, watch out for the safety of the person measuring.

Things to Bring Along

We encourage you to bring this book along as a resource. But if you want to bring only a section, we suggest that you make copies of the scoring sheet in appendix 4 to take out in the field. A clipboard will help keep scoring sheets together and give you a writing surface. Chalk can also be useful for marking the bounds of your study area.

What Is Your Study Area?

Urban design qualities are observed at a human scale. They are measured over the length of an average city block or a portion of a block you might find in the suburbs. Although you can apply this manual to almost any street, our methodology has been tested and refined on urban streets and therefore works best on urban streets that have at least some commercial uses. A street with soaring skyscrapers in downtown works with this manual and so does a street going through a small village center with a coffee shop and drug store.

After you pick the general area you want to assess, you then need to establish the boundaries of the study area. Typically. your study area will be one block in length. In some cases, if you are assessing a long block, walk about 120 paces. This is about 300 feet, or the size of a small city block. In these cases, where you will not walk the entire block, marking off 120 paces with a piece of chalk will help. Remember, you will be walking the study area several times to make measurements.

Knowing What to Count

Some urban design qualities are related primarily to what is in your immediate surroundings, while other urban design qualities depend more on the entire environment you can see. Consequently, for some measurements, you will be instructed to count elements only on the same side of the street, whereas for others you will count on both sides of the street. Sometimes you will be instructed to count only elements that are physically located within the study area, and sometimes you will count elements that you can see from the study area.

Pay close attention to the specific instructions for each element. Instructions and scoring sheets will indicate which sides of the street you should measure ("your side" or "both sides") and also whether you should consider objects beyond the space you walked ("within study area" or "beyond study area"). Consider "within study area" to be anything within the area you walked or anything that is no more than 50 feet ahead of the area you walked. Consider "beyond study area" to be anything that is no more than 500 feet from the area you walked.

Map of the Field Manual

The instructions for measuring each urban design quality follow the same format. We first provide a short and concise definition (*what it is*) of each of the urban design qualities we suggest measuring. This definition is based on the urban design literature and was refined with the help of our expert panel of urban designers and top professionals from related fields (see chapters 2 and 3). We then provide a short description (*what it looks like*). Here we elaborate a little more on the types of features you may expect to see for each of the urban design qualities.

Finally, we describe the necessary steps to measure the physical features that we have found to have a strong relationship with each urban design quality. Measuring urban design qualities involves visiting streets and being able to identify and count certain street features. You will also need to make educated estimates of other features. Each procedure consists of steps, definitions, notes, and example illustrations that will help you measure physical features in a consistent and reliable way. Each procedure also concludes with a list of common questions and answers.

Steps are the ordered instructions that must be followed to make each measurement. The first step will always be to walk the entire length of your study area. Steps will also establish whether you will consider features on "your side" or "both sides" of the street and whether you will consider features "within [the] study area" or "beyond [the] study area." Refer back to the "Knowing What to Count" section to refresh your understanding of these terms.

After the steps, definitions are provided for key terms found within the steps. For example, a step may instruct you to count "small planters." The definitions section will go over what is meant by small planters.

Illustrations will help familiarize you with the concepts presented in each step. They will show examples of features you should consider in your measurement as well as examples of features you should not.

Notes will sometimes be found in between the steps, definitions, or questions. Notes will help clarify procedures or help explain illustrations.

But I Don't Know What or How to Measure!

The purpose of the field manual is to make measuring urban design qualities a simple task. Our instructions will help you to make rough measurements, which is all that is needed. Our research has shown that simple observations like the ones you will be making are sufficient to make valid and reliable assessments of urban design qualities. Do not become frustrated if you fail to count an object or cannot measure the exact dimensions of a feature. Just make sure your estimates seem reasonable and consistent with the other measurements you make!

Urban Design Quality Definitions

Imageability

What it is: The quality of a place that makes it distinct, recognizable, and memorable.

What it looks like: When specific physical elements and their arrangement complement one another, capture attention, evoke feelings, and create a lasting impression. Architecture that suggests importance, presence of historical buildings, and landmarks are the qualities of a place with high imageability.

Enclosure

What it is: The degree to which streets and other public spaces are visually defined by buildings, walls, trees, and other vertical elements.

What it looks like: The space has a roomlike quality. The height of vertical elements is proportionally related to the width of the space between them. The buildings become the "walls" of the outdoor room. The street and sidewalk become the "floor."

Human Scale

What it is: Size, texture, and articulation of physical elements that match the size and proportions of humans and correspond to the speed at which humans walk.

What it looks like: Buildings that include structural or architectural components of sizes and proportions that relate to the human form. Plentiful street furniture aimed at pedestrians.

Transparency

What it is: The degree to which people can see or perceive human activity or what lies beyond the edge of a street or other public space.

What it looks like: The passerby has the ability to see human activity, or signs thereof, beyond the street edge.

Complexity

What it is: The visual richness of a place that depends on the variety of the physical environment, including the numbers and kinds of buildings, architectural diversity and ornamentation, street furniture, and human activity.

What it looks like: Complex spaces have varied building shapes, sizes, materials, colors, architecture, ornamentation, and setbacks; many windows and doors; and varied lighting; they are highly populated.

Measurement Instructions

Imageability—*quality of a place that makes it distinct, recognizable, and memorable.*

Step 1: Count courtyards, plazas, and parks. Both sides, within study area.

- Walk the length of the block.
- As you walk, count instances of (not elements or sections of) courtyards, plazas, and parks on both sides.
- Record the number of courtyards, plazas, or parks you encountered within the study area.

Definitions:

- Courtyard: a permanent space in which people are intended and able to enter.
- Plaza: large, enterable open space (bigger than 15 square feet), often with art and plants, or associated with building(s).
- Park: place intended for human use/recreation; often with greenery, a playground, and so forth.
- Garden: enterable and larger than 10 square feet.
- *Note:* All features are accessible.

Examples:

Figures 6.1–6.4 illustrate examples of courtyards, plazas, or parks.

Figure 6.1. A plaza between two buildings with public art across the street.

Figure 6.2. A courtyard with tables and seating.

Figure 6.3. A plaza with flag-poles in the foreground and public art in the distance.

Figure 6.4. A small park across the street with benches.

Question:

- **Q.** Do manicured median strips count?
  A. No. Median strips, even those with seating, do not count.

Step 2: Count major landscape features. Both sides, beyond study area.

Directions:

- Walk the length of the block.
- Looking at both sides of the street and in the distance (only visible and prominent features ahead), count instances of individual/distinct natural landscape elements.
- Record the number of distinct landscape elements you encountered on either side of the street or in the distance (prominent distant features only).

Definitions:

- Major landscape features: prominent natural landscape views like bodies of water, mountain ranges, or human-made features that incorporate the natural environment; serve as natural landmarks for orientation or reference. Parks do not count as major landscape features.

Examples:

Figures 6.5 and 6.6 show examples of what can be considered major landscape features on the street. Figure 6.7 shows an example of what cannot. Use the figures to familiarize yourself with the scope of features that may count as major landscape features.

Figure 6.5. A marina—YES. A marina is a human-made feature that incorporates a natural landscape feature (water) and therefore would count as a major landscape feature.

Figure 6.6. A harbor—YES. Although mostly developed, the harbor shown here still incorporates the natural environment and would count as a major landscape feature.

Figure 6.7. A skyline—NO. A view of a city skyline may be quite prominent. However, since it does not incorporate natural elements, it would not count as a major landscape feature.

Questions:

- **Q.** Does a skyline count? (see examples)
  A. Simply a skyline is not enough to qualify; there also needs to be other natural elements.
- **Q.** If you know the feature is there but do not see it, does it still count?
  A. No. If the feature is not visible walking in the designated direction on the specified block, there are no major landscape features.

Step 3: Estimate the proportion of historic buildings. Both sides, within study area.

Directions:

- Walk the entire length of the block, looking at both sides.
- Estimate the proportion of historic buildings visible at street level (out of total block length excluding cross streets).

- Record the estimate as a decimal using increments of tenths (0.10).

Definitions:

- Historic: clearly determined to be pre–World War II: high detailing, dumbbell shape, iron fire escape, and so forth; post–World War II buildings are usually geometrically and architecturally simple (though they may be impressive), have lots of glass surface area, and little detailing.

Examples:

Figures 6.8–6.11 show a progression of views down both sides of one street.

Figure 6.8.   The right side of the street is entirely made up of modern glass and concrete structures.

Figure 6.9.   The left side of the street is entirely occupied with older buildings made of brick and stone. This street has approximately 50% of its building frontage, on the two sides, occupied by historic structures.

Figure 6.10.   The right side of the street is entirely made up of modern glass and concrete structures.

Figure 6.11.   The left side of the street is entirely occupied with older buildings made of brick and stone. This street has approximately 50% of its building frontage, on the two sides, occupied by historic structures.

Questions:

- **Q.** What if the building has more than one construction date?
  A. We are primarily concerned with street level. If there is more than one construction date for the street-level section of the building and the historic elements are still apparent, consider the building historic.
- **Q.** What if I can't tell if the building is historic?
  A. If there is no clear indicator that the building is historic, then you cannot count it as such.

Step 4: Count buildings with identifiers. Both sides, within study area.

Directions:

- Walk the length of the block.
- Count the buildings on both sides with identifiers that are visible from the sidewalk/path.
- Record the number of buildings with identifying features within the study area.

Definitions:

- Identifiers: clear signs or universal symbols that reveal a building's street-level use. A steeple can identify a church; gas pump, a gas station; tables and chairs, a restaurant; mannequins, a clothing store; and so forth. Words can also identify a lot or building: *high school*, *restaurant*, *pharmacy*, *shoe store*, *café*, and brand or franchise names. A name such as "Joe's" would not work, while "Joe's Pub" would identify the building.
- *Note:* If a single building has multiple street-level occupants, it is identifiable only if the majority of occupants are identifiable.

Examples:

Figures 6.12–6.14 show different examples of buildings with identifiers.

Figure 6.12.   A large building with several occupants with identifiable uses. The building in this figure will count as one building with identifiers since it is one building with many uses that can be identified with business signs.

Figure 6.13.   Three buildings with identifiers. The three buildings across the street are all identified by storefront signs that can be read.

Figure 6.14.   A church steeple in the distance. The steeple in the distance indicates the presence of a church; therefore, the church can count as a building with an identifier if it is within the study area.

Questions:

- **Q.** Are residential buildings identifiable?
  A. Unless there is a visible sign or symbol that clearly identifies the residence (doormen do not signify residences), the building is unidentifiable. (*Apartments, manor, condos, flats, tenements, co-ops,* and so forth are all words that if present on a sign on the building signify residential use.)
- *Note:* Many buildings have been converted and appearance is not reliable.
- **Q.** What if the building has a clear sign but it obviously no longer serves the advertised purpose or is vacant?
  A. If you know beyond a reasonable doubt that the building is either

vacant or does not serve its specified use, the building is not identifiable. Faded signs, boards, and/or paper covering windows are indicators that a storefront, or building, is vacant.

- **Q.** Does a "for rent" sign count?
  A. If the building exists (all walls up) and there is a sign that says "for rent," "coming soon," or "space for lease" where the function (land use) is specified, it is identifiable.

Step 5: Count buildings with nonrectangular shapes. Both sides, within study area.

Directions:

- Walk the length of the street.
- Count buildings with nonrectangular shapes on both sides.
- Record the number of buildings with nonrectangular shapes you counted within the study area. If the building is ambiguous, take a picture.

Definitions:

- Buildings with nonrectangular shapes: those that do not have simple rectangular profiles from at least one angle, as seen by the passing pedestrian. Visible pitched roofs, bay windows in the roof or foundation lines, dormers, and so forth qualify buildings as nonrectangular. Signs, awnings, entrances, and porches are not considered in the shape of the building.

Examples:

Figures 6.15–6.18 show examples of buildings with rectangular and nonrectangular shapes.

Figure 6.15.   One nonrectangular building. The building trim on the right-most building deviates enough from an otherwise rectangular shape to be considered nonrectangular.

Figure 6.16.   Two nonrectangular buildings. The pitched roofs and chimneys make the two right-most buildings nonrectangular.

Figure 6.17.   Three rectangular buildings. These modern skyscrapers all have simple rectangular shapes.

Figure 6.18.   One nonrectangular building. While the office building shown does not have any curved edges and comprises all right angles, it does not have a simple box shape.

Questions:

- **Q.** What if the building is made up of multiple rectangles?
  A. If you can see more than one rectangle, the building is not rectangular from at least one angle: count the building as nonrectangular.
- **Q.** What if the building has a water tower on top of it?
  A. If there are any structures incorporated into the building that give it a nonrectangular shape, consider the building nonrectangular. Take a picture if you are completely unsure.

Step 6: Record outside dining. Your side, within study area.

Directions:

- Walk the length of the block.
- Note the presence (1) or absence (0) of commercial or public outdoor dining on your side.
- Record a 1 if outdoor dining is present and a 0 if it is not.

Definitions:

- Outdoor dining: dining tables and seating located mostly or completely outside. Even if there are no patrons, there is outdoor dining as long as the tables and chairs are present.

Examples:

Figures 6.19–6.22 show examples of what can and cannot be considered outdoor dining.

Figure 6.19. Open outdoor dining with no patrons—YES. Although the tables are not being utilized, this place would be considered outdoor dining.

Figure 6.20. Closed outdoor dining—NO. The outdoor dining shown here has closed umbrellas and chairs on top of tables. This would not be considered outdoor dining.

Figure 6.21.   Open outdoor dining
with patrons—YES. These two places
have outdoor dining with patrons.
Count each even though one is partially
enclosed.

Figure 6.22.   Open outdoor dining
with patrons—YES. These two places
have outdoor dining with patrons.
Count each even though one is partially
enclosed.

Questions:

- **Q.** What if the outdoor dining is closed?
  A. If it looks as if the dining could be in operation at some point during
  the day, count the presence of outdoor dining.

Step 7: Count people. Your side, within study area.

Directions:

- Walk down the block at a reasonable pace.
- Count only visible people within the study area coming toward you,
  passing you, and those you pass. Also, count those who are walking no
  more than 10 feet ahead of you on the block. At the end of the block,
  count people on the cross street that are within 10 feet of you. Make
  sure not to count anyone twice.
- Walk the block (back and forth) a total of four times.
- Record the number of people you counted on each walk-through.
- You may compute the average number of people when you return to
  the office.
- *Note:* Do not count people who are seated at outdoor dining areas.

Definitions:

- Visible people: includes people walking, running, biking, standing, or
  sitting—everyone except those at outdoor dining.

Questions:

- **Q.** Do you count children and babies in strollers or backpacks?
  A. Yes, do count every person.

Step 8: Estimate noise level. Both sides, within study area.

Directions:

- Walk down the block at a reasonable pace.
- Evaluate the level of noise (1 = very quiet, 2 = quiet, 3 = normal, 4 = loud, 5 = very loud).
- Record your noise level rating.

Definitions:

- Noise: cars, trucks, sirens, people, music, construction, and so forth will all add to noise level.

> **Enclosure**—*the degree to which streets and other public spaces are visually defined by buildings, walls, trees, and other vertical elements.*

Step 1: Count long sight lines. Both sides, beyond study area.

Directions:

- Walk the entire length of the block.
- As you walk. count the number of directions (front, right, and left) in which you see at least one long sight line at any point along the block (0 min, 3 max). Do not count views down cross streets on ends of blocks.
- Record a 1 if you had a long sight line in one direction, a 2 for two directions, and a 3 if you had a long sight line in all three directions at least once during your walk-through.
- *Note:* Do not force it. Long sight lines should be visible without strain.

Definitions:

- Long sight line: the ability to see at least 1,000 feet or about three city blocks into the distance at any point during your walk through the block.

Examples:

Figures 6.23–6.25 show street scenes with and without long sight lines. Use these figures to help you identify where long sight lines can occur.

Figure 6.23.   A long sight line down the street—1. The lack of an enclosed environment where this shot was taken (low-rise buildings, open plaza on right, wide avenue) allows you to see far ahead.

Figure 6.24.   Sight lines blocked—0. The regular spacing of mature street trees blocks your view of the block ahead.

Figure 6.25.   A long sight line across the street—1. The ill-defined street wall across the street allows you to see buildings far into the distance.

Questions:

- **Q.** Does it count if you can see some distant sky through the trees?
  A. Only count it if the view is not significantly obstructed. Widely spaced trees may allow for long sight lines.
- **Q.** What if the block is on a downhill slope?
  A. If there is a long sight line due to the incline or elevation of the block, count it.
- **Q.** What if you can see through the frame of a building that is being constructed?
  A. Do not count sight lines through buildings.

Step 2A and 2B: Estimate the proportion of street wall. A—your side, within study area (10 feet); B—opposite side, within study area (10 feet).

Directions:

- Walk the length of the block.
- Note the proportion of your side of the block that consists of a street wall (of the total block length). Do the same for the opposite side of the street (excluding the cross streets from the denominator).
- Record the proportion estimates (use decimal increments of 0.10) for your side and the opposite side (two measurements).

Definitions:

- Street wall: the effect achieved when structures on a block continuously front the sidewalk/path providing a defined street-edge and feeling like a wall. A facade or wall over 5 feet contributes to the street wall if it is set back no more than 10 feet from the sidewalk/path edge. Gates/fences, greenery, or both over 5 feet tall that obstruct more than 60 percent of your view of the space beyond also count. Lawns, lots, driveways, and alleys break the street wall.
- *Note:* Construction sites with solid partitions over 5 feet (and within 10 feet of the sidewalk/path edge) add to the street wall. If lots under construction are not blocked off and present enough information (all walls), code the block imagining the structure(s)-to-be. If you cannot determine the structure of an open lot (not enough of it built yet), there is no street wall.

Examples:

Figures 6.26–6.28 show a progression of views down one street. Use the figures to help you estimate the proportion of street wall.

Figure 6.26.   No street wall. The parking lot on the right side of the street does not provide a defined edge to the street and therefore does not contribute to the street wall.

Figure 6.27.   Transition to a street wall. As you walk farther down the street, the building ahead fronts along the sidewalk and provides a defined street edge.

Figure 6.28.   Transition back to an ill-defined edge. Past the building, the street wall again deteriorates into a parking lot.

The estimated street wall for the right side of this street would be 20 percent. In other words, 20 percent of the street length has buildings fronting the sidewalk with setbacks of less than 10 feet.

Questions:

- **Q.** Do cross streets break the street wall?
  A. No. Cross streets do not count as breaks in the street wall.
- **Q.** What about brownstones with stairs coming down to the sidewalk?
  A. If brownstones are set back no more than about 10 feet, they create a street wall.
- **Q.** Do fences or walls add to the street wall?
  A. If the fence is over 5 feet tall and obstructs more than 60 percent of the view overall, it contributes to the street wall.

Step 3A and 3B: Estimate the proportion of sky. A—ahead, beyond study area; B—across, beyond study area.

Directions:

- Look directly ahead.
- Without moving your head, assess the percentage of sky visible in your frame of vision.
- Record the estimated proportion (use decimal increments of 0.05).
- Do the same, this time looking across the street, directly to your left. Make sure you are standing at the beginning of the block just past the cross street.
- *Note:* Sky visible through a glass obstruction does not count as visible sky.

Definitions:

- Frame of vision: your frame of vision is the "box" that is visible when you look ahead with your line of sight parallel to the ground. To better define the area, make a box with your fingers (thumbs and pointer fingers) and hold it up to your face. Slowly move it away until you can see all four sides—this is your box.

Examples:

Figures 6.29–6.32 will help you visualize different proportions of sky ahead and across the street.

Figure 6.29.   10% sky ahead.

Figure 6.30.   20% sky across.

Figure 6.31. 30% sky ahead.   Figure 6.32. 40% sky across.

Questions:

- **Q.** What if the building to my left is under construction?
  A. If it is under construction, there is an obstructed view and therefore
  the proportion of the sky you can see will be smaller.

Step 4: Record street trees. Both sides, within study area.

Directions:

- Walk the length of the block.
- Note the presence of street trees on both sides of the street and on the
  median strip (if one is present).
- Circle the letter in the box that corresponds to the location of the street
  trees; leave it blank if there are none. Y = your side, O = opposite side,
  M = median strip.

Human scale—*the size, texture, and articulation of physical elements
that match the size and proportions of humans and, equally important,
correspond to the speed at which humans walk.*

Step 1: Identify long sight lines. Both sides, beyond study area.

Directions:

- Same rules apply as for Enclosure step 1. Use that measurement. Do not
  measure twice.

Step 2: Estimate the proportion of windows at street level. Your side, within study area.

Directions:

- Walk the length of the block.
- Note the proportion of street-level facade on your side that is covered by windows of any size.
- Record the proportion out of the whole block length (use decimal increments of 0.10) that is covered by street-level windows.

Examples:

Figures 6.33–6.36 show a progression of views down one street. Blue highlighted areas indicate where windows are present. Gray highlighted areas indicate portions of buildings that are not at street level.

Overall, this street has an estimated 70 percent of street-level building surface area made up of windows.

Figure 6.33.

Figure 6.34.

Figure 6.35.

Figure 6.36.

Questions:

- **Q.** Do sunken or raised first-floor windows count?
  A. Include only the windows at street level. The windows should be oriented to the eye level of passing pedestrians.
- **Q.** Do windows in buildings under construction count?
  A. If the building is being constructed behind a partition or does not have all of its walls yet, windows do not exist for the lot. Buildings that are being maintained or renovated and are not behind solid construction partitions have windows.
- **Q.** If the windows are cloudy, are made of reflective glass, or the curtains are drawn, are they included?
  A. Yes. Street-level windows are at the scale of and intended for humans and give the impression that there is activity beyond or within the building and should count.

Step 3: Estimate average building height. Your side, within study area.

Directions:

- Walk the length of the study block.
- Note the height of the buildings on your side, whether they are set back, and the percentage of the block that the buildings of the same height occupy.
- On the reverse side of the form, record the heights of the buildings (record buildings of the same height together), considering their width, the total length of the block, and thus the percentage of the block (adding to 100 percent) each building height spans.
- You may wait to compute the average later after you return from the field.
- *Note:* If there are no buildings, there is a zero height.

Definitions:

- Building height: height in feet, assuming 10 feet per floor, including the roof floor of buildings with slanted roofs and dormers and any visible sunken floors.
- Setback: buildings that move back from the street as their height increases or buildings that are farther than 20 feet from the sidewalk/path edge.

Examples:

Figures 6.37–6.40 show a progression of views down one street. Use the figures to help you estimate average building height.

Figure 6.37.   First-floor retail occupies the bottom levels of the first two buildings. The first floors are approximately 10 feet.

Figure 6.38.   Taller second stories are found on the first two buildings. These floors are about 15 feet. The total height for the first two buildings is about 25 feet.

Figure 6.39.   A two-story residential building with a basement occupies the remainder of the street on our side.

Figure 6.40.   A closer view of the residential building reveals that the two levels are partially above street level (approximately 4 feet). The two residential floors are approximately 8 feet each. The total height is approximately 20 feet.

The average building height shown in the progression of views done on this street is approximately 24 feet.

Questions:

- **Q.** What if you cannot discern the number of floors from your vantage point either because the building is too tall or because the floors are not easily identifiable?

A. Record "200 feet" if you know the building is over 20 floors and you cannot make a better estimate.

- **Q.** What if the building has different heights?
  A. Count to the highest floor of the building.
- **Q.** What if you can't tell where one floor starts and the next begins?
  A. If you can see the complete height, try using a building with a known height near it as a guide (e.g., it is twice the height of the building with 15 floors; therefore, it has 30 floors).
- *Note:* Make sure to document the percentage of the total block length the building occupies.

Step 4: Count small planters. Your side, within study area.

Directions:

- Walk the length of the block.
- Count all the visible street-level planters on your side of the block and within 10 feet of the sidewalk edge. This includes planters on private and public property but not those inside enclosed parks or gardens.
- Record the total number of small planters on your side, within the study area.

Definitions:

- Small planters: any potted arrangement of trees, shrubs, or flowers that are smaller than 10 square feet at their base. The planter should be within 10 feet of the sidewalk edge and appear to be permanent (not small enough to be able to be brought inside at the end of the day) but not inground.

Examples:

Figures 6.41–6.44 show examples of what can and cannot be considered small planters.

Figure 6.41.   A small flowerbed next to a window. A small planter can be a part of a building as long as the flowerbed appears to be less than 10 square feet.

Figure 6.42.   Two small planters by a large planting bed. The two small planters are large enough that they are permanent aspects of the streetscape. The planting bed in the background is too large to be considered.

Figure 6.43.   A small planter behind a streetlight. This small planter appears just large enough that it is probably a permanent fixture of the streetscape.

Figure 6.44.   Flower pots that are too small. The pots along the storefront can be easily taken indoors anytime; therefore, they will not be considered small planters.

Questions:

- **Q.** If the plants in the pot are dead, do I still count the planter?
  A. Count the planter even if the plants are dead because there is the intention of a planter.
- **Q.** What if the planter is on a porch or set back from the sidewalk?
  A. If the planter is located no higher than 10 feet from and no lower than the street level, it counts.
- **Q.** What if the planter is behind a fence?

A. If you can see the planter, it is less than 10 feet from the sidewalk edge, and it is not within an enclosed park or garden, you may count it.

Step 5A: Count street furniture and other street items. Your side, within study area.

Directions:

- Walk the length of the block.
- Count visible street furniture and other items on your side and within the block. Do not count furniture in enclosed parks, gardens, plazas, and courtyards.
- Record the total number if it is under 40; record "40+" if over.
- *Note:* Do not count tables and chairs for outdoor dining. These will be counted separately. However, if chairs are not associated with outdoor tables (they are alone), count each chair or stack of chairs. Where there are both stacked tables and chairs, count each table only.

Step 5B: Count outdoor dining tables. Your side, within study area.

Directions:

- Walk the length of the block.
- Count the number of outdoor tables for dining on your side and within the study area.
- Record the number of tables you count.
- *Note:* These are tables with associated chairs or benches.

Step 5C: Count other lights. Your side, within study area.

Directions:

- Walk the length of the block.
- Count the number of pedestrian lights no more than 10 feet above ground level.
- Record the number of lights you encounter.

Definitions:

- Street furniture and other street items: only the following: tables (without associated chairs), chairs (without associated tables), vendor displays (count one per vendor), ATMs, hanging plants, benches, flower pots, parking meters, umbrellas, trash cans (public only), newspaper boxes, mailboxes, bike racks, bollards (count one per set), hydrants, flags, banners, merchandise stands, street vendors, pedestrian-scale street lights (not for cars), phone booths (one per structure), bus stops (count one per stop), and train stations (count one per entrance).

- Other lights: outdoor lights that are not on poles; usually attached to a building facade or lining the side of a path.

Examples:

Figures 6.45–6.47 show examples of what can be considered as street furniture and other street items.

Figure 6.45. Two street items (green outlines)—grouping of small flowerpots that are too small to be counted as small planters, and a trash can. Five outdoor dining tables.

Figure 6.46. Six street items— 1–3: parking meters, 4: trash can, 5: ATM, 6: pedestrian-scale streetlight. One other light (green outline): light attached to a store entrance.

Figure 6.47. Three street items— 1: street banner, 2: pedestrian-scale streetlight, 3: bench. One other light (green outline): a lantern attached to a building.

Questions:

- **Q.** What does not count?
  A. If the object is on the list, count it. Objects such as construction materials, streetlights, parking and traffic signs, and garbage bags sitting on the curb do not count.
- **Q.** Do furniture displays (retail furniture) count?
  A. Yes, they do count.
- **Q.** What if there are over 40 pieces of street furniture?
  A. Do not count all the items; simply record "40+."
- **Q.** What if there are no chairs associated with the tables but the tables are clearly intended for outdoor dining?
  A. If there are no chairs because they have all been moved elsewhere on the sidewalk to accommodate a party, the chairs are still associated and you can count the tables. If the chairs are stacked or if there are no chairs, count the tables as street furniture (5A), as well as each stack of chairs (5A).
- **Q.** What if two or more tables have been brought together?
  A. Two tables brought together can be counted as one; more than that, count separately.

Transparency—the degree to which people can see or perceive what lies beyond the edge of a sidewalk/path or public space and, more specifically, the degree to which people can see or perceive human activity beyond the edge of a street or other public space.

Step 1: Estimate the proportion of windows at street level. Your side, within study area.

Directions:

- The same rules apply as for Human Scale step 2. Use that measurement. Do not measure twice.

Step 2: Estimate the proportion of street wall. Your side, within study area.

Directions:

- The same rules apply as for Enclosure Step 2A. Do not measure twice.

Step 3: Estimate the proportion of active uses. Your side, within study area.

Directions:

- Walk the length of the block.
- Note the amount of active-use buildings that are on your side within the study area. If a building is active, assume all sides are active (even blank walls).
- Record the proportion of the total block (use decimal increments of 0.10).

Definitions:

- Active use building: one in which there is frequent pedestrian traffic (more than 5 people enter/exit while you are observing the block).
- Always active: parks, stores, restaurants, attached/apartment-style residential buildings, hospitals, and schools.
- Always inactive: construction sites, parking lots, churches, detached/ single residence units, and vacant or abandoned lots.

Examples:

Figures 6.48–6.51 show a progression of views down one street. Green highlighted areas indicate active uses while red highlighted areas indicate inactive uses.

Figure 6.48. (1) inactive use—office with no apparent activity, (2) active use—restaurant with on street dining, (3) active use—street-oriented retail. This street has approximately 60% of its street frontage devoted to active uses.

Figure 6.49. (1) inactive use—office with no apparent activity, (2) active use—restaurant with on-street dining, (3) active use—street-oriented retail. This street has approximately 60% of its street frontage devoted to active uses.

Figure 6.50. (1) inactive use—office with no apparent activity, (2) active use—restaurant with on-street dining, (3) active use—street-oriented retail. This street has approximately 60% of its street frontage devoted to active uses.

Figure 6.51. (1) inactive use—office with no apparent activity, (2) active use—restaurant with on-street dining, (3) active use—street-oriented retail. This street has approximately 60% of its street frontage devoted to active uses.

Questions:

- **Q.** If you do not know the building's use, how do you assess the activity?

  A. If the building appears to be residential, look for signs that indicate people live there (mailboxes, buzzers, window treatments, etc.). If you cannot conclude that it is residential or if the building is an unknown nonresidential building, watch the pedestrian traffic during the time you are measuring the block and record the building as active if more than 5 people enter or exit while you are observing the block.

- *Note:* Residential buildings may not be identifiable as defined under imageability, but if the building can be assumed to be residential, it can be considered active.

Complexity—the visual richness of a place that depends on the variety of the physical environment, specifically the numbers and kinds of buildings, architectural diversity and ornamentation, landscape elements, street furniture, signage, and human activity.

Step 1: Count buildings. Both sides, within study area.

Directions:

- Walk the length of the block.
- Count the visible buildings on both sides of the street within the study area.
- Record the number of buildings within the study area.
- *Note:* This includes corner lot buildings and all buildings that are enterable from the study area only.

Definitions:

- Visible buildings: buildings that can be distinguished by separate doors/entrances (especially for residential), architecture, colors, and so forth.

Examples:

Figures 6.52–6.56 show a progression of views down one street. Use the figures to help you determine which buildings are within your immediate area or are prominent enough to be counted.

Figure 6.52.

Figure 6.53.

Figure 6.54.

Figure 6.55.

Figure 6.56.

Questions:

- **Q.** Is a sidewalk or path in front of brownstones only one building?
  A. Remember, this is about complexity. If the brownstones can be distinguished by different doors, different colors, different ornamentation, and so forth, count them individually.

Step 2A: Count basic building colors. Both sides, within study area.

Directions:

- Walk the length of the block.
- Count the number of basic building/structure/surface colors on both sides of the street within the study area. Do not distinguish between different shades of the same color.
- Record the number of distinct building colors.

Step 2B: Count building accent colors. Both sides, beyond study area (10 feet).

Directions:

- Walk the length of the block.
- Count the number of accent colors used on either side of the street and within the study area.
- Record the number of distinct accent colors.

Definitions:

- Basic color: the color used for the majority of the building's facade.
- Accent color: the color used for building trims and roofs, street objects, awnings, signs, and so forth.

Examples:

Figures 6.57–6.60 show street scenes with different numbers of basic and accent colors.

Figure 6.57.   Basic building colors: 2 (tan, red brick). Accent colors: 2 (red, green).

Figure 6.58.   Basic building colors: 1 (off-white). No accent colors.

Figure 6.59. Basic building colors: 1 (orange). Accent colors: 2 (tan, green).

Figure 6.60. Basic building colors: 3 (brown, white, red brick). Accent colors: 2 (green, brown).

Questions:

- **Q.** What if there is more than one basic color on a single building? **A.** If one color is the overwhelming majority, count only that color; if both colors are significant, count the two colors separately.
- **Q.** If the accent color is the same as the basic color, does it still count? **A.** No. If the building is one color, it has no accent color.

Step 3: Record outdoor dining. Your side, within study area.

Directions:

- The same rules apply as for Imageability step 6. Use that measurement. Do not measure twice.

Step 4: Count public art. Your side, within study area.

Directions:

- Walk the length of the block.
- Count individual pieces of public art that are within the study area or intended for viewing from the sidewalk/path.
- Record the number of pieces of public art.

Definitions:

- Public art: monuments, sculptures, murals, and any artistic display that has free access. Art must be the size of a small person or have clear identification indicating its status as art (creator, dedication, year, materials, etc.).

Examples:

Figures 6.61–6.64 show examples of public art.

Figure 6.61.   A sculpture fountain.

Figure 6.62.   A stone monument.

Figure 6.63.   A sculpted figure.

Figure 6.64.   A piece of modern art.

Questions:

- **Q.** What if the art is clearly on someone's property?
  A. If the art is visible to the passing pedestrian, it has free access and it can be considered public art.
- **Q.** What if the art is incorporated into a building facade?
  A. If the art can be isolated as a specific artistic element of a facade, the building counts as one instance of public art.
- **Q.** How small or simple can the art be?
  A. It should be semipermanent, be intended for the viewing of others, and add to the visual appeal and complexity of the block. Small fountains and graffiti murals would be included, but simple chalk drawings and graffiti tags would not be included.

Step 5: Count pedestrians. Your side, within study area.

Directions:

- The same rules apply as for Imageability step 7. Use that measurement.
  Do not measure twice.

Biosketches of Expert Panel Members

Victor Dover is a principal of Dover, Kohl & Partners, founded in 1987 and based in South Miami, Florida. Mr. Dover earned his bachelor of architecture degree from Virginia Tech and his master's degree in town and suburb design from the University of Miami. He has been certified by the American Institute of Certified Planners and is a charter member of the Congress for the New Urbanism. Mr. Dover and his partner Mr. Kohl have been recognized by *Architecture* magazine as being "among the country's best architects and urban designers."

Geoffrey Ferrell established his own urban design firm in 1992. Before that, Mr. Ferrell worked as a designer/code writer for Duany-Plater-Zyberk Architects and Town Planners in Miami and as the director of urban design for the Treasure Coast Regional Planning Council in Florida. He holds a master of architecture degree with a certificate in American urbanism from the University of Virginia, a bachelor of architecture from Oregon School of Design, and a bachelor of science in public policy from Willamette University. Mr. Ferrell is a charter member of the Congress for the New Urbanism. His work is featured in the book *The New Urbanism* by Peter Katz (McGraw-Hill, 1994).

Mark Francis is professor of landscape architecture at the University of California, Davis, where he founded and directed the Center for Design Research. Trained in landscape architecture and urban design at Berkeley and Harvard, his work is concerned with the design and theory of urban places. He is associate editor of the *Journal of Architectural and Planning Research* and serves on the editorial boards of several journals, including *Landscape Journal, Environment and Behavior, Journal of Planning Literature,* and *Children and Youth Environments.* His most recent books are *Urban Open Space* (Island Press, 2003) and *Village Homes* (Island Press, 2003).

Michael Kwartler is the founding director of the Environmental Simulation Center, a nonprofit research laboratory created to develop innovative applications of information technology for community planning, design, and decision making. He conceived and directed the design and development of CommunityViz™, the first GIS-based planning decision support software to fully integrate virtual reality with scenario design, impact analysis, and policy simulation. He was made a fellow of the American Institute of Architects in 1990 for his achievements in urban design and performance zoning.

Robert Lane is the director of the Regional Design Program and the Healthy Communities Initiative at the Regional Planning Association of New York and New Jersey. Mr. Lane is the author of numerous urban design studies and town plans that emphasize compact mixed-use development, alternative forms of mobility, and other dimensions of active living community design. Robert Lane is also the coprincipal investigator on several "natural experiments," including measuring the impacts on activity levels of a new greenway in Stamford, Connecticut, and of new transit services in New Jersey.

Anne Vernez Moudon is professor of architecture, landscape architecture, and urban design and planning at the University of Washington, Seattle. She is president of the International Seminar on Urban Morphology (ISUF), a faculty associate at the Lincoln Institute of Land Policy, a fellow of the Urban Land Institute, a national advisor to the Robert Wood Johnson Foundation, and an active participant in the Mayors' Institute on City Design. Dr. Moudon holds a bachelor of architecture from the University of California, Berkeley, and a doctor of science from the Ecole Polytechnique Fédérale of Lausanne, Switzerland. Her published works include *Built for Change: Neighborhood Architecture in San Francisco* (MIT Press, 1986), *Public Streets for Public Use* (Columbia University Press, 1991), and *Monitoring Land Supply with Geographic Information Systems* (with M. Hubner; Wiley, 2000).

Anton Nelessen is founder and president of the award-winning firm A. Nelessen Associates. He served as consultant on seven of the ten Smart Growth awards given by the State of New Jersey. Mr. Nelessen has been a professor at Harvard University and at the Rutgers University Department of Urban Planning and Policy Development since 1974. His trademarked Visual Preference Survey has been used to generate comprehensive plans, master plans, and specific urban design plans all over the United States. Mr. Nelessen is a charter member of the Congress for the New Urbanism. His book *Visions for a New American Dream* was published by the American Planning Association (1994). His current book, *What People Want*, is in first draft.

John Peponis is a professor at the School of Architecture, Georgia Institute of Technology. He has pioneered the development of computational descriptions of the spatial organization of buildings and cities as it affects their human performance. He is a leading researcher and scholar in the field of space syntax. His work addresses equally the fundamental principles and constraints that govern the generation and functions of built form and the application of research in design practice, to help set design aims and evaluate design alternatives. He collaborates regularly with Kokkinou and Kourkoulas Architects, based in Greece, and has been involved in the design of the Michaniki office complex in Marousi, the Benaki-Pireos Museum, The Shop and Trade mixed-use complex, and other projects. His research has been funded by the National Science Foundation, the General Services Administration, Steelcase, the Georgia

Tech Foundation, and, more recently, Perkins + Will, with whom he collaborates on developing new tools for the assessment of the human performance of architecture and urban design. His papers have appeared in *Environment and Planning B*, *Environment and Behavior*, the *Journal of Architecture*, and *Urban Design International*. For more information, see http://www.coa.gatech.edu/people/john-peponis..

Michael Southworth is professor in both the Department of City and Regional Planning and the Department of Landscape Architecture and Environmental Planning at the University of California, Berkeley. Trained and professionally registered in both city planning and architecture, he received the PhD and MCP degrees from the Massachusetts Institute of Technology, and the bachelor of architecture and bachelor of arts from the University of Minnesota. He is a fellow of the American Institute of Architects and a member of the American Institute of Certified Planners. His recent books include *Streets and the Shaping of Towns and Cities* (with Eran Ben-Joseph; Island Press, 2003), *City Sense and City Design* (as editor and contributor with Tridib Banerjee; MIT Press, 1990), and *Wasting Away* (as contributor; by Kevin Lynch; Sierra Club Books, 1990).

Daniel Stokols is professor of Planning, Policy, and Design and dean emeritus of the School of Social Ecology at the University of California, Irvine. Dr. Stokols received his bachelor degree at the University of Chicago and his master and doctorate degrees at the University of North Carolina, Chapel Hill. He is past president of the Division of Population and Environmental Psychology of the American Psychological Association. Dr. Stokols was a recipient of the Annual Educator Award from the International Facility Management Association in 1988, the Annual Career Award of the Environmental Design Research Association in 1991, and the UCI Lauds and Laurels Faculty Achievement Award in 2003.

Operational Definitions of Physical Features

Variable Long Name and Type	Counting Criteria	Measurement Protocol
Variable Long Name: courtyards/plazas/ parks—both sides *Variable Type:* count	Pass camera or within 50 feet, both sides	Count individual courtyards, plazas, and parks that the camera passes on either side of the street or that are within 50 feet from the camera. Large parks that occupy a whole block will still count as one park.
Variable Long Name: arcade—same side *Variable Type:* dummy 1 = yes, 0 = no	None	Indicate the presence of an arcade. An arcade will be defined as a covered passageway that allows the passageway to be protected from rain and direct sun while retaining the advantages of an outdoor space. Count arcades regardless of whether the camera is inside or outside the arcade.
Variable Long Name: landmarks—both sides *Variable Type:* count	20% screen height, both sides	Count the number of landmarks. A landmark must be at least 20% of the screen height. A landmark is defined as a building or structure that stands out from the background buildings. The structure should be prominent or well-known enough that it could plausibly be used as a reference point for orientation and for providing directions to visitors.
Variable Long Name: types of landmarks *Variable Type:* text	None	List the landmarks counted.
Variable Long Name: major landscape features—both sides *Variable Type:* count	20% screen height, both sides	Count the views of mountain ranges, bodies of water, and other human-made features that incorporate the surrounding environment (e.g., a marina) that would serve as natural landmarks. The major landscape feature should be prominent or well known enough that it could plausibly be used as a reference point for orientation and for providing directions to visitors. The feature should occupy at least 20% of the screen height.

Variable Long Name and Type	Counting Criteria	Measurement Protocol
Variable Long Name: types of major landscape features *Variable Type:* text	None	List the major landscape features counted.
Variable Long Name: memorable architecture *Variable Type:* dummy 1 = yes, 0 = no	Counted buildings	Indicate the presence of memorable architecture. This is defined as more than just well-designed buildings. Memorable architecture implies that the scene as a whole contains architecture that makes the scene prominent or well known. The scene as a whole could plausibly be used as a reference point for orientation and for providing directions to visitors. A well-known landmark can serve as memorable architecture.
Variable Long Name: buildings with memorable architecture *Variable Type:* text	None	List buildings that contribute to the scene having memorable architecture.
Variable Long Name: distinctive signage *Variable Type:* dummy 1 = yes, 0 = no	20% screen height, both sides; or passed, or within 50 feet, same side	Indicate the presence of distinctive signage. A sign is distinctive if it is prominent or well known enough that it could be plausibly used as a reference point for orientation and for providing directions to visitors. The occurrences of distinctive signage should occupy at least 20% of the screen height or be within 50 feet of the camera.
Variable Long Name: occurrences of distinctive signage *Variable Type:* text	None	List instances where distinctive signage occurs.
Variable Long Name: long sight lines *Variable Type:* count	1,000 feet ahead	Indicate the number of directions in which the camera can see far into the distance. Maximum number is 3 (right, left, front). "Far into the distance" will be defined as seeing at least 1,000 feet into the distance.
Variable Long Name: terminated vista *Variable Type:* dummy 1 = yes, 0 = no	20% screen height	Indicate whether the street the camera travels along is terminated with a building or a feature that blocks distant views. The feature that blocks distant views must occupy at least 20% of the screen height.

Variable Long Name and Type	Counting Criteria	Measurement Protocol
Variable Long Name: progress toward next intersection *Variable Type:* proportion	Minimum 0.05	Estimate how far the camera has traveled in relation to the end of the block. Instances where a street that intersects with the opposite side of the street but not with the side where the camera is traveling (a t-intersection) will not be considered the end of the block if the intersecting street appears to be minor (fewer than 2 marked lanes, no signalization, no marked crosswalks). Enter 0.05 if the next intersection is not visible. Use 0.10 intervals otherwise.
Variable Long Name: proportion of distance walked versus distance visible *Variable Type:* proportion	Minimum 0.05	Estimate how far the camera has traveled in relation to the most distant feature seen. Enter 0.05 if the distance beyond seems infinite. Use 0.10 intervals otherwise. Use the same value as you progress toward the next intersection if the farthest distance visible is the end of the block.
Variable Long Name: street connections to elsewhere *Variable Type:* count	None	Count visible street connections. The camera must be able to see down the street or pedestrian way to count as a connection to elsewhere.
Variable Long Name: number of buildings – both sides *Variable Type:* count	20% screen height, both sides	Count buildings along the street and in the distance that occupy at least 20% of screen height. Large structures that are subdivided count as one building.
Variable Long Name: number of land uses—both sides *Variable Type:* count	20% screen height, both sides	Count different land uses observed on both sides of the street. Land use distinctions are civic/community, residential, lodgings, office, medical, retail (includes restaurants and shops), entertainment, transit station, and park. Parking, even in a structure, will not be considered a land use. Only count land uses from features that occupy at least 20% of screen height or from buildings that have been counted.
Variable Long Name: types of land uses *Variable Type:* text	None	List the land uses counted.
Variable Long Name: proportion of historic building frontage—both sides *Variable Type:* proportion	Counted buildings, and fronting along street and passed or 500 feet ahead, both sides	Estimate the proportion of the street that is fronted by buildings that are historic. Architecture that can be determined to have originated from the World War II era or before will be considered historic. Relevant frontage is defined as the total distance the camera travels plus an additional 500 feet ahead from the end of the video clip.

Variable Long Name and Type	Counting Criteria	Measurement Protocol
Variable Long Name: types of historic buildings *Variable Type:* text	None	Identify the buildings in the scene that are historic.
Variable Long Name: number of buildings with identifiers— both sides *Variable Type:* count	Counted buildings, and fronting along street and passed or 500 feet ahead, both sides	Count the buildings whose use can be determined by building features. For example, a church can be identified by a steeple. Stores can be identified by signs that can be easily read in the video clip. If a building has been subdivided by several occupants, only count the building as identifiable if a majority of the occupants' uses can be determined by building features.
Variable Long Name: proportion of building frontage with identifiers *Variable Type:* proportion	Counted buildings, and fronting along street and passed or 500 feet ahead, both sides	Determine the building frontage whose uses can be determined by building features. Relevant frontage is defined as the total distance the camera travels plus an additional 500 feet ahead from the end of the video clip.
Variable Long Name: various building ages *Variable Type:* dummy 1 = yes, 0 = no	At least one counted building from different period	Indicate whether buildings appear to have been built at different time periods. At least one counted building must appear to be built in a different time period.
Variable Long Name: number of primary building materials *Variable Type:* count	Counted buildings	Count different primary building materials for buildings that have been counted. Glass counts as a building material only if it makes up the entire building.
Variable Long Name: types of primary building materials *Variable Type:* text	None	List the counted building materials.
Variable Long Name: number of dominant building colors *Variable Type:* count	Counted buildings	Count the different dominant building colors for buildings that have been counted. If the roof color of a building is different from the building color, the roof color will count as an accent color.
Variable Long Name: dominant building colors *Variable Type:* text	None	List the counted dominant building colors for buildings that have been counted.

Variable Long Name and Type	Counting Criteria	Measurement Protocol
Variable Long Name: number of accent colors—both sides *Variable Type:* count	Counted buildings, objects that occupy 20% of screen height or within 50 feet, both sides	Count the number of accent colors. Accent colors contrast with the dominant building colors and can come from street furniture, awnings, business signs, and building trim. Accent colors will be counted only from objects that meet one of the counting conventions. The object must occupy at least 20% of the screen height or be within 50 feet from the camera.
Variable Long Name: accent colors *Variable Type:* text	None	List the counted accent colors.
Variable Long Name: building projections—same side *Variable Type:* count	At least 5 feet, passed or 50 feet ahead, same side	Count the building projections (such as porches, stoops, marquees, decks, balconies, window bays, etc.) that project at least 5 feet from the building and are from buildings that have been counted, which front the street and which are passed or are within 50 feet from the camera at the end of the clip.
Variable Long Name: visible sets of doors—same side *Variable Type:* count	Passed or 50 feet ahead, same side	Count the sets of doors that the camera passes or that are within 50 feet from the camera on the same side of the street. Do not assume the location of doors or count doors seen in window reflections.
Variable Long Name: visible recessed doors—same side *Variable Type:* count	Counted doors	Count the number of recessed doorways of counted visible doorways. Doorways are recessed if they are set back at least 3 feet from the building facade.
Variable Long Name: proportion of counted sets of door that are recessed *Variable Type:* proportion	None	Divide the visible recessed doors by the visible sets of doors.
Variable Long Name: proportion of first-floor facade that has windows—same side *Variable Type:* proportion	Fronting along street, and passed or 50 feet ahead, and set back no more than 50 feet same side	Estimate the proportion of the first floor of buildings that front the street on the same side that are passed or are within 50 feet from the camera at the end of the clip that is window. Use 0.10 intervals.

Variable Long Name and Type	Counting Criteria	Measurement Protocol
Variable Long Name: proportion of entire facade that has windows—same side *Variable Type:* proportion	Fronting along street, and passed or 50 feet ahead, and set back no more than 50 feet same side	Estimate the proportion of the entire surface of buildings that front the street on the same side that are passed or are within 50 feet from the camera at the end of the clip that is window. Use 0.10 intervals.
Variable Long Name: common window proportions—both sides *Variable Type:* dummy 1 = yes, 0 = no	At least 80% of counted buildings fronting along street and passed or 500 feet ahead, both sides	Indicate whether windows have common proportions. Common window proportions occur when at least 80% of windows on all buildings are predominantly vertical or horizontal and have similar architectural trim. If a building on one of the sides has no window, then there are no common window proportions.
Variable Long Name: awnings or overhangs—both sides *Variable Type:* count	Counted buildings fronting along street and passed or 50 feet ahead, both sides	Count the number of awnings or overhangs on buildings that have been counted on both sides of the street and that are passed or are within 50 feet from the camera at the end of the clip.
Variable Long Name: height interruptions—same side *Variable Type:* proportion	Counted buildings fronting along street and passed or 50 feet ahead, same side	Estimate the proportion of building frontage that has been counted on the same side that front the street and is within 50 feet from the camera at the end of the video clip with belt courses or other visual interruptions to building height. One-story buildings should be considered as height interrupted. Use 0.10 intervals.
Variable Long Name: number of buildings with nonrectangular silhouettes *Variable Type:* count	Counted buildings	Count the buildings that have been counted whose shape is not a simple rectangular box. Pitched roofs on buildings that are viewed at an angle and make the building look nonrectangular do count as nonrectangular. Building roof trim that makes variations in an otherwise simple rectangular shape do also count as nonrectangular.
Variable Long Name: proportion of buildings with nonrectangular silhouettes *Variable Type:* proportion	None	Divide the number of buildings with nonrectangular silhouettes by the number of counted buildings.

Variable Long Name and Type	Counting Criteria	Measurement Protocol
Variable Long Name: common architectural style—both sides *Variable Type:* dummy 1 = yes, 0 = no	At least 80% of counted buildings fronting along street and passed or 500 feet ahead, both sides	Indicate the presence of common architectural styles. Common architectural styles occur when at least 80% of the counted buildings that front the street and that have been passed or are within 500 feet from the camera at the end of the video clip use similar architectural styles or have consistent building trim and roof pitch.
Variable Long Name: common materials— both sides *Variable Type:* dummy 1 = yes, 0 = no	At least 80% of counted buildings fronting along street and passed or 500 feet ahead, both sides	Indicate the presence of common building materials. Common building materials occur when at least 80% of the counted buildings that front the street and that have been passed or are within 500 feet from the camera at the end of the video clip use the same primary building material.
Variable Long Name: proportion of active uses—same side *Variable Type:* proportion	Counted buildings fronting along street and passed or 50 feet ahead, same side	Determine the proportion of street frontage that has active uses. Active uses are defined as shops, restaurants, public park, and other uses that generate significant pedestrian traffic. Inactive uses include blank walls, parking lots, vacant lots, abandoned buildings, and offices with no apparent activity. In regard to residential uses, when the density appears to be more than 10 units per acre, assume the land use to be active. The street frontage will be defined as the total distance traveled by the camera plus an additional 50 feet ahead from the end of the video clip.
Variable Long Name: proportion of street wall—same side *Variable Type:* proportion	Counted buildings fronting along street and passed or 500 feet ahead, same side	Determine the proportion of street that is occupied by a continuous wall or facade adjacent to the sidewalk. Facades set back by parking or lawn and driveways do not count as street wall. Intersecting streets and ends of blocks, however, should not count against street wall. The street will be defined as the total distance the camera travels plus an additional 500 feet ahead from the end of the video clip.
Variable Long Name: proportion of street wall—opposite side *Variable Type:* proportion	Counted buildings fronting along street and passed or 500 feet ahead, opposite side	Determine the proportion of the street that is occupied by a continuous wall or facade adjacent to the sidewalk. Facades set back by parking or lawn do not count as street wall. Driveways also do not count as street wall. Intersecting streets and ends of blocks, however, should not count against street wall. The street will be defined as the total distance the camera travels plus an additional 500 feet ahead from the end of the video clip.

Variable Long Name and Type	Counting Criteria	Measurement Protocol
Variable Long Name: enclosed sides *Variable Type:* count	At least 80% of frontage passed or 500 feet ahead that is blocked, both sides	Indicate the number of sides of the street that are enclosed. Maximum number is 3 (front, same side, opposite side). A side is considered enclosed if 80% of the frontage on that side is blocked by buildings or other features that are opaque at street level whether or not they front along the sidewalk. If the street is terminated by a vista, then the front is enclosed. Relevant frontage is defined as the total distance the camera travels plus an additional 500 feet ahead from the end of the video clip.
Variable Long Name: average building set-back from sidewalk or travel path—same side *Variable Type:* dimension	Passed on the same side or 50 feet ahead	Estimate the average setback of buildings from the sidewalk or travel path on the same side. Buildings that front directly on the sidewalk have a setback of 0.
Variable Long Name common setbacks—both sides *Variable Type:* dummy 1 = yes, 0 = no	No more than 30% variance for buildings fronting along street and passed or 500 feet ahead, both sides	Indicate whether buildings that have been counted, that front along the street, and that are within 500 feet from the camera at the end of the video clip have a common setback. Common setbacks occur when all building setbacks vary no more than 30%. Recessed courtyards and other small breaks in street wall that can be determined as part of a building do not negate the presence of common setbacks.
Variable Long Name: building height—same side *Variable Type:* dimension	Passed or 500 feet ahead, same side	Estimate the average building height of buildings on the same side of the street based on the proportion of street fronted by each building. Only estimate building heights for buildings that have been counted, that front along the street, and that are within 500 feet from the camera at the end of the video clip. Use 0 if there are no buildings that front along the street. Only estimate the height of a building that you can see if the camera does not pan the entire height of the building. Assume that the height for one typical floor is 10 feet.
Variable Long Name: building height to width ratio—same side *Variable Type:* ratio	Passed or 500 feet ahead, same side	Estimate the average width of buildings on the same side. Only estimate the ratio for buildings that have been counted, that front along the street, and that are within 500 feet from the camera at the end of the video clip. Divide the average height of buildings on the same side by the average width of buildings on the same side.

Variable Long Name and Type	Counting Criteria	Measurement Protocol
Variable Long Name: building height—opposite side *Variable Type:* dimension	Passed or 500 feet ahead, opposite side	Estimate the average height of buildings on the opposite side of the street. Only estimate building heights for buildings that have been counted, that front along the street, and that are within 500 feet from the camera at the end of the video clip. Use 0 if there are no buildings that front along the street. Only estimate the height of buildings that you can see if the camera does not pan the entire height of the building. Assume that the height for one typical floor is 10 feet.
Variable Long Name: common building heights—both sides *Variable Type:* dummy 1 = yes, 0 = no	No more than 30% variance for buildings fronting along street and passed or 500 feet ahead, both sides	Indicate whether buildings have common building heights. Common building heights occur when the height of all buildings that have been counted, that front along the street, and that are within 500 feet from the camera at the end of the video clip varies no more than 30%.
Variable Long Name: common building masses—both sides *Variable Type:* dummy 1 = yes, 0 = no	No more than 30% variance for buildings fronting along street and passed or 500 feet ahead, both sides	Indicate whether buildings have common building masses. Common mass occurs when the mass of all buildings that have been counted, that front along the street, and that are within 500 feet from the camera at the end of video clip varies no more than 30%.
Variable Long Name: street width *Variable Type:* dimension	Average of passed or 50 feet ahead	Estimate the street width. Street width includes frontage roads and parking aisles. Assume that a typical parking lane is 8 feet and a typical travel lane is 12 feet. If the median between a one-way pair is more than 50 feet wide, treat each couplet as separate streets. Only consider the width of the adjacent half street.
Variable Long Name: median width *Variable Type:* dimension	Average of passed or 50 feet ahead	Estimate the median width if one is present. Medians should be raised in order to be considered.
Variable Long Name: sidewalk width—same side *Variable Type:* dimension	Average of passed or 50 feet ahead, same side	Estimate the total sidewalk width. Estimate the average if the sidewalk width varies.

Variable Long Name and Type	Counting Criteria	Measurement Protocol
Variable Long Name: building height to street width ratio *Variable Type:* ratio	None	Street width is defined as the total width from building face to building face. If the building face to building face distance varies, estimate an average. Compute the average of building heights of both sides of street. Divide by the total width of the street, including street, median, sidewalks, and average setback from the sidewalk.
Variable Long Name: sidewalk clear width—same side *Variable Type:* dimension	Average of passed or 50 feet ahead, same side	Estimate the width of the sidewalk with no obstructions.
Variable Long Name: buffer width—same side *Variable Type:* dimension	Average of passed or 50 feet ahead, same side	Estimate the width from the outside clear width to moving cars (the distance between moving cars and the portion of the sidewalk where pedestrians are most likely to walk).
Variable Long Name: number of paving materials *Variable Type:* count	Passed or 50 feet ahead	Count the number of different paving materials for the street, the sidewalk on the same side, and the surfaces connected to the sidewalk on the same side. Paving material categories are asphalt, concrete, colored concrete, brick, paver, and aggregate.
Variable Long Name: types of paving materials *Variable Type:* text	None	List the counted paving materials.
Variable Long Name: textured sidewalk surface—same side *Variable Type:* dummy 1 = yes, 0 = no	Passed or 50 feet ahead, same side	Indicate the presence of a textured sidewalk. Textured sidewalks or streets are composed of materials that have patterns (brick, pavers, stamped asphalt, patterned or stamped concrete). The patterned materials usually resemble brick and are used to visually break up sidewalk or street. A sidewalk or street will be considered textured if at least 50% of the surface is textured.
Variable Long Name: textured street surface *Variable Type:* dummy 1 = yes, 0 = no	Passed or 50 feet ahead	Indicate the presence of a textured street. Textured sidewalks or streets are composed of materials that have patterns (brick, pavers, stamped asphalt, patterned or stamped concrete). The patterned materials usually resemble brick and are used to visually break up sidewalk or street. A sidewalk or street will be considered textured if at least 50% of the surface is textured.

Variable Long Name and Type	Counting Criteria	Measurement Protocol
Variable Long Name: pavement condition *Variable Type:* rating	Passed or 50 feet ahead	Rate the pavement condition on a 1–5 Likert scale taking note of visible cracks, discoloration, patches, presence of weeds, etc. Rate the condition of the sidewalk on the same side and the street.
Variable Long Name: pavement condition explanation *Variable Type:* text	None	Explain the pavement condition rating.
Variable Long Name: debris condition *Variable Type:* rating	Passed or 50 feet ahead	Rate the debris condition of pavement on a 1--5 Likert scale taking note of dirt, leaves, and trash. Rate the condition of the sidewalk on the same side and the street.
Variable Long Name: debris condition explanation *Variable Type:* text	None	Explain the debris condition rating.
Variable Long Name: parked cars—same side *Variable Type:* count	Passed or 50 feet ahead, same side	Count parked cars on the same side that are within 50 feet from the camera.
Variable Long Name: proportion of street with parked cars—same side *Variable Type:* proportion	Passed or 50 feet ahead, same side	Estimate the proportion of street frontage on the same side with parked cars. Make deductions for occupied parking spaces that are extra long. The relevant frontage is defined as the total distance the camera travels plus an additional 50 feet ahead from the end of the video clip.
Variable Long Name: moving cars—both sides *Variable Type:* count	Passed or 50 feet ahead, both sides	Count the number of cars that pass the camera on either side of that street or that are within 50 feet from the camera.
Variable Long Name: speed *Variable Type:* measurement	None	Estimate the speed of moving cars using 5 mph intervals.
Variable Long Name: traffic to street width ratio *Variable Type:* ratio	None	Divide the number of moving cars on both sides by the street width.

Variable Long Name and Type	Counting Criteria	Measurement Protocol
Variable Long Name: moving cyclists— both sides *Variable Type:* count	Passed or 50 feet ahead, both sides	Count the number of moving bicyclists on either side of the street or who are within 50 feet from the camera.
Variable Long Name: curb extensions— same side *Variable Type:* count	Passed or 50 feet ahead, same side	Count the curb extensions that are passed or that are within 50 feet from the camera. Curb extensions are extensions of the sidewalk into the street to facilitate shorter distances for pedestrians to cross and to slow down oncoming vehicular traffic. They can occur midblock or at intersections.
Variable Long Name: midblock crossings *Variable Type:* count	Passed or 50 feet ahead, same side	Count midblock crossings that are passed or that are within 50 feet from the camera. Midblock crossings are marked crossings for pedestrians that do not occur at street intersections.
Variable Long Name: midblock passage-ways—same side *Variable Type:* count	Passed or 50 feet ahead, same side	Count open passageways into street wall (such as alleys) that are passed or that are within 50 feet from the camera.
Variable Long Name: overhead utilities *Variable Type:* dummy 1 = yes, 0 = no	None	Indicate the presence of overhead utility lines.
Variable Long Name: number of landscape elements—both sides *Variable Type:* count	20% screen height, both sides; or within 50 feet, same side	Count each type of tree, bush, and visible ground-cover. Distinguish between trees in natural settings versus trees in wells or landscaped beds, evergreen trees versus deciduous, small trees versus tall trees. Note the occurrences of bushes or hedges and turf. Only count landscape elements that either occupy at least 20% of screen height or are within 50 feet from the camera.
Variable Long Name: type of landscape elements *Variable Type:* text	None	List the counted landscape elements.
Variable Long Name: landscaped median *Variable Type:* dummy 1 = yes, 0 = no	Passed or 50 feet ahead	Indicate the presence of a landscaped median. The median should be landscaped for more than 50% for the median that is passed and ahead 50 feet from the end of the clip.

Variable Long Name and Type	Counting Criteria	Measurement Protocol
Variable Long Name: number of trees—both sides *Variable Type:* count	20% screen height, both sides	Count the total number of trees on both sides that occupy at least 20% of screen height.
Variable Long Name: trees in wells or landscaped beds—same side *Variable Type:* count	At least 10 square feet and within 50 feet, same side	Count the number of trees that are in tree wells, well-landscaped adorned planting beds, or well-landscaped fenced areas that are at least 10 square feet and within 50 feet from the camera.
Variable Long Name: proportion of sidewalk shaded by trees—same side *Variable Type:* proportion	Passed or 50 feet ahead, same side	Estimate the proportion of sidewalk that is shaded by trees. The relevant sidewalk is defined as the total distance the camera travels plus an additional 50 feet ahead from the end of the video clip.
Variable Long Name: large planters without trees—same side *Variable Type:* count	At least 10 square feet and within 50 feet, same side	Count the number of large landscaping beds with shrubs or flowers that are more than 10 square feet and within 50 feet from the camera.
Variable Long Name: small planters—same side *Variable Type:* count	Less than 10 square feet and within 50 feet, same side	Count the number of small planting pots with shrubs or flowers that are less than 10 square feet and that are within 50 feet from the camera. Small planters should be permanent elements of the streetscape and not pots that are taken in at the end of the day. Do not count small planters that are indoors and can be seen through windows.
Variable Long Name: landscape condition *Variable Type:* rating+B7	Counted landscape elements	Rate the condition of the counted landscape elements on a 1–5 Likert scale taking note of upkeep and lack of adequate landscaping.
Variable Long Name: landscape condition reasons *Variable Type:* text	None	Explain the landscape condition rating.
Variable Long Name: common tree spacing and type—same side *Variable Type:* dummy 1 = yes, 0 = no	Passed or 500 feet ahead	Indicate the presence of common tree spacing and type on the same side of the street. Common tree spacing occurs when the spacing of trees varies by no more than 30%.

Variable Long Name and Type	Counting Criteria	Measurement Protocol
Variable Long Name: common tree spacing and type—both sides *Variable Type:* dummy 1 = yes, 0 = no	Passed or 500 feet ahead	Indicate whether the tree spacing and type on the opposite side of the street is common to the same side of the street. Common tree spacing occurs when the spacing of trees varies by no more than 30%.
Variable Long Name: moving pedestrians—same side *Variable Type:* count	Within 50 feet, same side	Count the moving pedestrians who are within 50 feet of the camera.
Variable Long Name: people standing still—same side *Variable Type:* count	Within 50 feet, same side	Count the people standing still who are within 50 feet of the camera.
Variable Long Name: people seated—same side *Variable Type:* count	Within 50 feet, same side	Count the people seated who are within 50 feet of the camera.
Variable Long Name: noise level *Variable Type:* Likert scale 1 = very quiet 5 = very loud	None	Estimate the noise level, taking note of noise from traffic, pedestrians, and any other ambient noises.
Variable Long Name: noise level explanation *Variable Type:* text	None	Explain the noise level rating.
Variable Long Name: outdoor dining—same side *Variable Type:* dummy 1 = yes, 0 = no	Within 50 feet, same side	Count the number of distinct places that provide outdoor dining. Count outdoor dining areas even if there are no diners. However, do not count outdoor dining if the dining area appears closed (umbrellas folded up, chairs on tables).
Variable Long Name: tables—same side *Variable Type:* count	Within 50 feet, same side	Count outdoor dining tables as well as other tables that are within 50 feet from the camera.
Variable Long Name: seats—same side *Variable Type:* count	Within 50 feet, same side	Count the number of seats that are within 50 feet from the camera. Seats around private dining do not count as seats. Only count public seating. Factor in seating on planters, walls, bus stops, and so forth.

Variable Long Name and Type	Counting Criteria	Measurement Protocol
Variable Long Name: types of seating *Variable Type:* text	None	Explain the number of seats counted. State how many seats come from planters, walls, and so forth.
Variable Long Name: pedestrian-scale streetlights—both sides *Variable Type:* count	20% screen height, both sides	Count the pedestrian-scale streetlights that are at least 20% of screen height. Pedestrian-scale streetlights are no more than 20 feet in height. They are oriented toward the pedestrian and are ornamented.
Variable Long Name: other street furniture—same side *Variable Type:* count	Within 50 feet, same side	Count the other pieces of street furniture within 50 feet from the camera. Count parking meters, trash cans, newspaper boxes, mailboxes, bike racks, bollards, other street lights, and so forth.
Variable Long Name: types of other street furniture—same side *Variable Type:* text	None	List the other pieces of street furniture counted.
Variable Long Name: miscellaneous street items—same side *Variable Type:* count	Within 50 feet, same side	Count the miscellaneous street items that are within 50 feet from the camera. Count hydrants, flags, banners, merchandise stands, street vendors, ATMs, hanging plants, flower pots, umbrellas, and so forth.
Variable Long Name: types of miscellaneous street items—same side *Variable Type:* text	None	List the miscellaneous street items counted.
Variable Long Name: public art—both sides *Variable Type:* count	20% screen height, both sides; or within 50 feet, same side	Count the pieces of public art (sculptures, murals, etc.) that occupy at least 20% of screen height.
Variable Long Name: traffic signs—same side or median *Variable Type:* count	Within 50 feet, same side	Count the street signs that are warning, regulatory, or directional for automobiles that are within 50 feet from the camera.
Variable Long Name: place/building/business signs—same side *Variable Type:* count	Within 50 feet, same side	Count freestanding, hanging, and wall-mounted signs that are outside buildings and that are within 50 feet from the camera. Lettering on buildings that is legible will count as building signs.

Variable Long Name and Type	Counting Criteria	Measurement Protocol
Variable Long Name: directional signage—same side *Variable Type:* count	Within 50 feet, same side	Count the directional signage oriented to the pedestrian that is within 50 feet from the camera.
Variable Long Name: billboards *Variable Type:* count	20% screen height, both sides; or within 50 feet, same side	Count the billboards that occupy at least 20% of screen height or that are within 50 feet from the camera.
Variable Long Name: common signage *Variable Type:* dummy 1 = yes, 0 = no	Counted signs	Indicate the presence of common signage. Common signage occurs when counted signs appear to have the same design.
Variable Long Name: graffiti *Variable Type:* dummy 1 = yes, 0 = no	20% screen height, both sides or within 50 feet, same side	Indicate the presence of graffiti.
Variable Long Name: view of sky ahead *Variable Type:* proportion	None	Pause the video at the initial view down the street. Estimate the proportion of screen that is sky. Estimate proportions in increments of 0.05.
Variable Long Name: view of buildings ahead *Variable Type:* proportion	None	Pause the video at the initial view down the street. Estimate the proportion of screen that is buildings. Estimate proportions in increments of 0.05.
Variable Long Name: view of pavement ahead *Variable Type:* proportion	None	Pause the video at the initial view down the street. Estimate the proportion of screen that is pavement. Estimate proportions in increments of 0.05.
Variable Long Name: view of cars ahead *Variable Type:* proportion	None	Pause the video at the initial view down the street. Estimate the proportion of screen that is cars. Estimate proportions in increments of 0.05.

Variable Long Name and Type	Counting Criteria	Measurement Protocol
Variable Long Name: view of street furniture ahead *Variable Type:* proportion	None	Pause the video at the initial view down the street. Estimate the proportion of screen that is street furniture. Pedestrian-scale streetlights, tables, seating, other street furniture, other miscellaneous street items, and public art all count as street furniture. Estimate proportions in increments of 0.05.
Variable Long Name: view of landscaping ahead *Variable Type:* proportion	None	Pause the video at the initial view down the street. Estimate the proportion of screen that is landscaping. Estimate proportions in increments of 0.05.
Variable Long Name: view of other ahead *Variable Type:* proportion	None	Pause the video at the initial view down the street. Estimate the proportion of screen that is occupied by elements that cannot be categorized as sky, buildings, pavement, cars, street furniture, or landscaping (for example, people, freestanding signs). Estimate proportions in increments of 0.05.
Variable Long Name: types of other ahead *Variable Type:* text	None	List the elements that were categorized as other ahead.
Variable Long Name: view of sky across *Variable Type:* proportion	None	Pause the video at the initial view across the street. Estimate the proportion of screen that is sky. Estimate proportions in increments of 0.05.
Variable Long Name: view of buildings across *Variable Type:* proportion	None	Pause the video at the initial view across the street. Estimate the proportion of screen that is buildings. Estimate proportions in increments of 0.05.
Variable Long Name: view of pavement across *Variable Type:* proportion	None	Pause the video at the initial view across the street. Estimate the proportion of screen that is pavement. Estimate proportions in increments of 0.05.
Variable Long Name: view of cars across *Variable Type:* proportion	None	Pause the video at the initial view across the street. Estimate the proportion of screen that is cars. Estimate proportions in increments of 0.05.

Variable Long Name and Type	Counting Criteria	Measurement Protocol
Variable Long Name: view of street furniture across *Variable Type:* proportion	None	Pause the video at the initial view across the street. Estimate the proportion of screen that is street furniture. Pedestrian-scale street lights, tables, seating, other street furniture, other miscellaneous street items, and public art all count as street furniture. Estimate proportions in increments of 0.05.
Variable Long Name: view of landscaping across *Variable Type:* proportion	None	Pause the video at the initial view across the street. Estimate the proportion of screen that is landscaping. Estimate proportions in increments of 0.05.
Variable Long Name: view of other across *Variable Type:* proportion	None	Pause the video at the initial view across the street. Estimate the proportion of screen that is occupied by elements that cannot be categorized as sky, buildings, pavement, cars, street furniture, or landscaping (for example, people, freestanding signs). Estimate proportions in increments of 0.05.
Variable Long Name: types of other across *Variable Type:* text	None	List the elements that were categorized as initial other across.
Variable Long Name: maximum value of view ahead *Variable Type:* proportion	None	Record the largest value of the view ahead variables.
Variable Long Name: maximum value of view across *Variable Type:* proportion	None	Record the largest value of the view across variables.

Urban Design Qualities and Physical Features

Hypothesized in regular type (x) and validated in bold (**X**)

Variable	Imageability	Legibility	Enclosure	Human Scale	Transparency	Linkage	Complexity	Coherence	Tidiness
Courtyards/plazas/parks—both sides	**X**		x		x		x		
Arcade—same side			x	x	x	x			
Landmarks—both sides	x	x							
Major landscape features—both sides	**X**	x							
Memorable architecture	x	**X**							
Distinctive signage	x	x							
Long sight lines			x	**X**	**X**	x			
Terminated vista	x	**X**	x	x		x			
Progress toward next intersection				x		x			
Proportion of distance walked versus distance visible				x		x			
Street connections to elsewhere			x			**X**			
Number of buildings—both sides							**X**		
Number of land uses—both sides							x		
Proportion of historic building frontage—both sides	**X**								
Number of buildings with identifiers—both sides	**X**	**X**							
Proportion of building frontage with identifiers									
Various building ages							x	x	

Variable	Imageability	Legibility	Enclosure	Human Scale	Transparency	Linkage	Complexity	Coherence	Tidiness
Number of primary building materials							x	x	
Number of dominant building colors	x						**X**	x	
Number of accent colors—both sides							**X**	x	
Building projections—same side						x	x		
Visible sets of doors—same side				x	**X**	**X**	x		
Visible recessed doors—same side									
Proportion of counted sets of doors that are recessed						**X**			
Proportion of first-floor facade with windows				**X**	x				
Proportion of entire facade with windows				x	**X**				
Common window proportions—both sides								**X**	
Awnings or overhangs—both sides			x	x		x	x		
Height interruptions—same side				x					
Number of buildings with nonrectangular silhouettes	**X**						x		
Proportion of buildings with nonrectangular silhouettes	x								
Common architectural style both sides						x		x	
Common materials—both sides								x	
Proportion of active uses—same side				**X**	**X**		x		
Proportion of street wall—same side			**X**		**X**				
Proportion of street wall—opposite side			**X**						
Enclosed sides			x						
Average building setback					x				
Common setbacks—both sides			x					x	
Building height—same side			x	**X**	x				
Building height to width ratio—same side				x					
Building height—opposite side			x	x					

Variable	Imageability	Legibility	Enclosure	Human Scale	Transparency	Linkage	Complexity	Coherence	Tidiness
Common building heights—both sides			x			X		x	
Common building masses—both sides								x	
Street width			x	x		x			
Median width				x					
Sidewalk width—same side					x				
Building height to street width ratio			x						
Sidewalk clear width—same side				x					
Buffer width—same side				x					
Number of paving materials							x	x	
Textured sidewalk—same side				x		x	x		
Textured street				x		x	x		
Pavement condition									X
Debris condition									X
Parked cars—same side						x			
Proportion of street with parked cars—same side			x	x					
Moving cars—both sides				x		x	x		
Speed				x					
Traffic to street width ratio				x					
Moving cyclists—both sides				x			x		
Curb extensions—same side				x		x	x		
Midblock crossings				x		x	x		
Midblock passageways—same side				x	x	x	x		
Overhead utilities							x		X
Number of landscape elements—both sides							x		
Landscaped median				x		x	x		
Number of trees—both sides			x	x			x		

Variable	Imageability	Legibility	Enclosure	Human Scale	Transparency	Linkage	Complexity	Coherence	Tidiness
Trees in wells or landscaped beds—same side				x			x		
Proportion of sidewalk shaded by trees—same side			x						
Large planters without trees—same side				x			x		
Small planters—same side				**X**			x		
Landscape condition									**X**
Common tree spacing and type—same side		**X**						x	x
Common tree spacing and type—both sides		x				x		**X**	x
Pedestrians moving—same side	**X**			x			**X**	**X**	
Stationary people standing—same side	x			x			x		
People seated—same side	x			x	x		x		
Noise level	**X**			x			x		
Outdoor dining—same side	**X**			x	x	**X**	**X**		
Tables—same side				x			x		
Seats—same side				x			x		
Pedestrian-scale street lights—both sides			x	x			x	**X**	
Other street furniture—same side				x			x	x	x
Miscellaneous street items—same side				**X**			x		x
Public art—both sides	x	**X**		x			**X**		
Traffic signs—same side or median							x	x	x
Place/building/business signs—same side		**X**					x	x	x
Directional signage—same side		x					x		
Billboards	x			x			x		x
Common signage						x		x	
Graffiti							x		x
Sky ahead				**X**					
Buildings ahead				x					

Variable	Imageability	Legibility	Enclosure	Human Scale	Transparency	Linkage	Complexity	Coherence	Tidiness
Pavement ahead									
Cars ahead									
Street furniture ahead									x
Landscaping ahead			x						x
Sky across			**X**						
Buildings across			x						
Pavement across									
Cars across									
Street furniture across									x
Landscaping across			x						x
Maximum ahead							x		
Maximum across							x		

Scoring Sheet Measuring Urban Design Qualities

Measuring urban design qualities scoring sheet			auditor:			
street:		from:		to:		
block ID/face num.:		date & time:		weather/temp:		
Step #	Quality	Step	Process	Direction	Study area	Recorded value
Imageability						
1.1	imageability	accessible courtyards, plazas, parks, and gardens	count	both sides	within	
1.2	imageability	visible/prominent major landscape features	count	both sides	beyond	
1.3	imageability	proportion historic building/block (exclude thru st.)	est. (.10)	both sides	within	
1.4	imageability	buildings with identifiers	count	both sides	within	
1.5	imageability	buildings with nonrectangular shapes	count	both sides	within	
1.6	imageability	presence of outdoor dining	Y=1/N=0	your side	within	
1.71	imageability	people walk-through 1	walk-through	your side	within	
1.72		walk-through 2				
1.73		walk-through 3				
1.74		walk-through 4				
1.75		Total/4				
1.8	imageability	noise level (1–5; 5 is loudest)	est. (1–5)	both sides	within	
Enclosure						
2.1	enclosure	long sight lines (0–3)	count	both sides	beyond	
2.21	enclosure	proportion of street wall	est. (0.10)	your side	within	
2.22	enclosure	proportion of street wall (exclude thru st)	est. (0.10)	opposite side	within	

2.31	enclosure	proportion of sky	est. (0.05)	ahead	beyond	
2.32	enclosure	proportion of sky	est. (0.05)	across	beyond	
2.4	enclosure	street trees (Y = your side, O = opposite, M = median)	presence	both sides	within	Y O M
Human Scale						
3.1	human scale	long sight lines (0–3)	—	both sides	beyond	
3.2	human scale	proportion window (street-level)/block	est. (0.10)	your side	within	
3.3	human scale	building height	average	your side	within	
3.4	human scale	small planters	Count	your side	within	
3.51	human scale	pieces of street furniture & other street items	Count	your side	within	
3.52	human scale	outdoor dining tables	Count	your side	within	
3.53	human scale	lights on buildings (not more than 10 ft. high)	Count	your side	within	
Transparency						
4.1	transparency	proportion window (street-level)/block	—	your side	within	
4.2	transparency	proportion street wall	—	your side	within	
4.3	transparency	proportion active use/block	est. (0.10)	your side	within	
Complexity						
5.1	complexity	buildings	count	both sides	within	
5.21	complexity	basic building colors	count	both sides	within	
5.22	complexity	accent colors	count	both sides	within	
5.3	complexity	presence of outdoor dining	—	your side	within	
5.4	complexity	pieces of public art	count	both sides	within	
5.51	complexity	people walk-through 1	—	your side	within	
5.52		walk-through 2				
5.53		walk-through 3				
5.54		walk-through 4				
5.55		Total/4				

Buildings: Number (5.1), Nonrectangular (1.5), Historic (1.3), Identified (1.4), & Active (4.3)

| | Your side, buildings | | | | | | Opposite side, buildings | | | |
						(% must equal 100)				(% must equal 100)
	Nonrec	Historic	ID	1 fl actv	Height	Street %:	Nonrec	Historic	ID	Street %:
1										
2										
3										
4										
5										
6										
7										
8										
9										
10										
11										
12										
13										
14										
15										
16										
17										
18										
19										
20										
21										
22										
23										
24										
25										
26										
27										
28										
29										
30										

Building Colors (5.21 and 5.22)

Check off the primary building and building accent colors you see on both sides of the street

	Building	Accent
Red		
Orange		
Yellow		
Green		
Blue		
Purple		
Pink		
Brown		
Gray		
White		
Black		
Gold		
Silver		

References

Active Living by Design (ALbD). 2012. "Active Living by Design: Increasing Physical Activity and Healthy Eating through Community Design." http://www.active livingbydesign.org.

Alexander, C. 1965. "A City Is Not a Tree." *Architectural Forum* 122 (April): 58–62.

Alexander, C., S. Ishikawa, and M. Silverstein. 1977. *A Pattern Language: Towns, Buildings, Construction*. New York: Oxford University Press.

American Heritage Dictionary of the English Language. 2006. 4th ed. Boston: Houghton Mifflin.

Appleyard, D. 1969. "Why Buildings Are Known." *Environment and Behavior* 1:131–56.

———. 1981. *Liveable Streets*. Berkeley: University of California Press.

Arlington County (VA). 2003. *Columbia Pike Form Based Code (Section 20. Appendix A of the Zoning Ordinance)*. http://www.columbiapikeva.us/ revitalization-story/columbia-pike-initiative/columbia-pike-form-based-code.

Arnheim, R. 1977. *Dynamics of Architectural Form*. Berkeley: University of California Press.

Arnold, H. 1993. *Trees in Urban Design*. New York: Van Nostrand Reinhold.

Bacon, E. 1974. *Design of Cities*. New York: Viking.

Badland, H., S. Opit, K. Witten, R. Kearns, and S. Mavoa. 2010. "Can Virtual Streetscape Audits Reliably Replace Physical Streetscape Audits?" *Journal of Urban Health* 87 (6): 1007–16.

Badoe, D. A., and E. J. Miller. 2000. "Transportation–Land-Use Interaction: Empirical Findings in North America, and the Implications for Modeling." *Transportation Research D* 5 (4): 235–63.

Ball, K., A. Bauman, E. Leslie, and N. Owen. 2001. "Perceived Environmental Aesthetics and Convenience and Company Are Associated with Walking for Exercise among Australian Adults." *Preventive Medicine* 33 (5): 434–40.

Blumenfeld, H. 1953. "Scale in Civic Design." *Town Planning Review* 24 (April): 35–46.

Boarnet, M., K. Day, M. Alfonzo, A. Forsyth, and J. M. Oakes. 2006. "The

Irvine-Minnesota Inventory to Measure Built Environments: Reliability Tests." *American Journal of Preventive Medicine* 30 (2): 153–59.

Brownson, R. C., J. J. Chang, A. A. Eyler, B. E. Ainsworth, K. A. Kirtland, B. E. Saelens, and J. F. Sallis. 2004. "Measuring the Environment for Friendliness toward Physical Activity: A Comparison of the Reliability of 3 Questionnaires." *American Journal of Public Health* 94 (3): 473–83.

Brownson, R. C., C. M. Hoehner, K. Day, A. Forsyth, and J. F. Sallis. 2009. "Measuring the Built Environment for Physical Activity: State of the Science." *American Journal of Preventive Medicine* 36 (4, Supp. 1): S99–S123.e112.

Cao, X., P. L. Mokhtarian, and S. L. Handy. 2009. "Examining the Impacts of Residential Self-Selection on Travel Behaviour: A Focus on Empirical Findings." *Transport Reviews* 29 (3): 359–95.

Carnegie, M. A., A. Bauman, A. L. Marshall, M. Mohsin, V. Westley-Wise, and M. L. Booth. 2002. "Perceptions of the Physical Environment, Stage of Change for Physical Activity, and Walking among Australian Adults." *Research Quarterly for Exercise and Sport* 73 (2): 146.

Carr, L. J., S. I. Dunsiger, and B. H. Marcus. 2011. "Validation of Walk Score for Estimating Access to Walkable Amenities." *British Journal of Sports Medicine* 45:1144–48.

Caughy, M. O., P. J. O'Campo, and J. Patterson. 2001. "A Brief Observational Measure for Urban Neighborhoods." *Health and Place* 7 (3): 225–36.

Centers for Disease Control and Prevention. 2010. "About Healthy Places." http://www.cdc.gov/healthyplaces/about.htm.

Cervero, R. 2003. "The Built Environment and Travel: Evidence from the United States." *European Journal of Transport and Infrastructure Research* 3 (2): 119–37.

City of Davis (CA). 2007. "Davis Downtown and Traditional Residential Neighborhood Design Guidelines." Appendix: 129. http://community-development.cityofdavis.org/media/default/documents/pdf/cdd/planning/forms/downtown-and-traditional-residential-neighborhoods-design-guidelines.pdf.

City of Denver (CO). 1993. *Streetscape Design Manual* (p. 46). http://www.denvergov.org/Portals/646/documents/DesignGuidelines_StreetscapeDesign_1993.pdf.

City of Glendale (CA). 2011. *Comprehensive Design Guidelines* (ch. 1.1, p. 2).

City of Raleigh (NC). 2002. "Urban Design Guidelines." In *Raleigh Comprehensive Plan*: 3-5.31. http://www.raleighnc.gov/business/content/PlanUrbanDesign/Articles/RaleighUrbanDesignCenter.html.

City of San Jose (CA). 2004. "Downtown Design Guidelines" (p. 69). http://www.sanjoseca.gov/DocumentCenter/Home/View/427.

City of Seattle (WA). 2004. "Urban Design Glossary."

Clarke, P., J. Ailshire, R. Melendez, M. Bader, and J. Morenoff. 2010. "Using

Google Earth to Conduct a Neighborhood Audit: Reliability of a Virtual Audit Instrument." *Health & Place* 16 (6): 1224–29.

Clemente, O., R. Ewing, S. Handy, and R. Brownson. 2005. *Measuring Urban Design Qualities—An Illustrated Field Manual*. Princeton, NJ: Robert Wood Johnson Foundation. http://www.activelivingresearch.org/downloads/fieldma nual_071605.pdf.

Clifton, K. J., A. Livi-Smith, and D. A. Rodriguez. 2007. "The Development and Testing of an Audit for the Pedestrian Environment." *Landscape and Urban Planning* 80 (1/2): 95–110.

Crane, R. 2000. "The Influence of Urban Form on Travel: An Interpretive Review." *Journal of Planning Literature* 15 (1): 3–23.

Cullen, G. 1961. *The Concise Townscape*. London: Reed Educational and Professional Publishing.

Duany, A., and E. Plater-Zyberk. 1992. "The Second Coming of the American Small Town." *Wilson Quarterly* 16:19–48.

Dumbaugh, E., and R. Rae. 2009. "Safe Urban Form: Revisiting the Relationship between Community Design and Traffic Safety." *Journal of the American Planning Association* 75 (3): 309–29.

Duncan, D. T., J. Aldstadt, J. Whalen, S. J. Melly, and S. L. Gortmaker. 2011. "Validation of Walk Score® for Estimating Neighborhood Walkability: An Analysis of Four US Metropolitan Areas." *International Journal of Environmental Research and Public Health* 8:4160–79.

Elshestaway, Y. 1997. "Urban Complexity: Toward the Measurement of the Physical Complexity of Streetscapes." *Journal of Architectural and Planning Research* 14:301–16.

ESRI. 2009. "ArcGIS Network Analyst." http://www.esri.com/software/arcgis/exten sions/networkanalyst.

Evans, G. W., C. Smith, and K. Pezdah. "Cognitive Maps and Urban Form." *Journal of the American Planning Association* 48 (2): 232–44.

Ewing, R. 1996. *Pedestrian- and Transit-Friendly Design*. Tallahassee: Florida Department of Transportation.

———. 2000. "Asking Transit Users about Transit-Oriented Design." *Transportation Research Record* 1735:19–24.

———. 2005. "Can the Physical Environment Determine Physical Activity Levels?" *Exercise and Sport Sciences Review* 33 (2): 69–75.

Ewing, R., and Cervero, R. 2001. "Travel and the Built Environment: A Synthesis." *Transportation Research Record* 1780: 87–114.

———. 2010. "Travel and the Built Environment—a Meta-Analysis." *Journal of the American Planning Association* 76 (3): 265–94.

Ewing, R., M. Greenwald, M. Zhang, J. Walters, M. Feldman, R. Cervero, L. Frank, and J. Thomas. 2011. "Traffic Generated by Mixed-Use Developments—A Six-Region Study Using Consistent Built Environmental Measures." *Journal of Urban Planning and Development* 137 (3): 248–61.

Ewing, R., and S. Handy. 2009. "Measuring the Unmeasurable: Urban Design Qualities Related to Walkability." *Journal of Urban Design* 14 (1): 65–84.

Ewing, R., S. Handy, R. C. Brownson, O. Clemente, and E. Winston. 2006. "Identifying and Measuring Urban Design Qualities Related to Walkability." *Journal of Physical Activity and Health* 3 (Supp. 1): S223–S240. http://www.activeliving research.org/node/10177.

Ewing, R., M. King, S. Raudenbush, and O. Clemente. 2005. "Turning Highways into Main Streets: Two Innovations in Planning Methodology." *Journal of the American Planning Association* 71:269–82.

Ewing, R., R. Schieber, and C. Zegeer. 2003. "Urban Sprawl as a Risk Factor in Motor Vehicle Occupant and Pedestrian Fatalities." *American Journal of Public Health* 93:1541–45.

Eyler, A. A., R. C. Brownson, S. J. Bacak, and R. A. Housemann. 2003. "The Epidemiology of Walking for Physical Activity in the United States." *Medicine and Science in Sports and Exercise* 35 (9): 1529–36.

Federal Highway Administration. 2009. "National Household Travel Survey." http://nhts.ornl.gov.

Fleiss, J. L. 1981. *Statistical Methods for Rates and Proportions*. 2nd ed. New York: Wiley.

Gehl, J. 1987. *Life between Buildings: Using Public Space*. New York: Van Nostrand Reinhold.

Giles-Corti, B., and R. J. Donovan. 2002. "Socioeconomic Status Differences in Recreational Physical Activity Levels and Real and Perceived Access to a Supportive Physical Environment." *Preventive Medicine* 35 (6): 601–11.

———. 2003. "Relative Influences of Individual, Social Environmental, and Physical Environmental Correlates of Walking." *American Journal of Public Health* 93 (9): 1583–89.

Greene, W. H. 2012. *Econometric Analysis*. New York: Prentice Hall.

Handy, S. 1992. "Regional versus Local Accessibility: Variations in Suburban Form and the Effects on Nonwork Travel." PhD diss. (unpublished), University of California, Berkeley.

———. 2005. "Critical Assessment of the Literature on the Relationships among Transportation, Land Use, and Physical Activity." In *Does the Built Environment Influence Physical Activity? Examining the Evidence*. Special report 282. Washington, DC: Transportation Research Board and Institute of Medicine

Committee on Physical Activity, Health, Transportation, and Land Use.

Handy, S. L., M. G. Boarnet, R. Ewing, and R. E. Killingsworth. 2002. "How the Built Environment Affects Physical Activity: Views from Urban Planning." *American Journal of Preventive Medicine* 23 (2, Supp. 1): 64–73.

Heath, G. W., R. C. Brownson, J. Kruger, R. Miles, K. E. Powell, L. T. Ramsey, and the Task Force on Community Preventive Services. 2006. "The Effectiveness of Urban Design and Land Use and Transport Policies and Practices to Increase Physical Activity: A Systematic Review." *Journal of Physical Activity and Health* 3 (1): 55–76.

Heath, T., S. Smith, and B. Lim. 2000. "The Complexity of Tall Building Facades." *Journal of Architectural and Planning Research* 17 (3): 206–20.

Hedman, R. 1984. *Fundamentals of Urban Design*. Chicago: American Planning Association.

Herzog, T. R., S. Kaplan, and R. Kaplan. 1982. "The Prediction of Preference for Unfamiliar Urban Places." *Population and Environment* 5 (1): 43–59.

Herzog, T. R., and O. L. Leverich. 2003. "Searching for Legibility." *Environment and Behavior* 35:459–77.

Hilbe, J. M. 2011. *Negative Binomial Regression*. Cambridge: Cambridge University Press.

Humpel, N., N. Owen, D. Iverson, E. Leslie, and A. Bauman. 2004. "Perceived Environment Attributes, Residential Location, and Walking for Particular Purposes." *American Journal of Preventive Medicine* 26 (2): 119–25.

Im, S. 1984. "Visual Preferences in Enclosed Urban Spaces: An Exploration of a Scientific Approach to Environmental Design." *Environment and Behavior* 16 (2): 235–62.

Jacobs, A. 1993. *Great Streets*. Cambridge, MA: MIT Press.

Jacobs, A., and D. Appleyard (1987). "Toward an Urban Design Manifesto." *Journal of the American Planning Association* 53:112–20.

Jacobs, J. 1961. *The Death and Life of Great American Cities*. New York: Random House.

Kaplan, R., and S. Kaplan. 1989. *The Experience of Nature: A Psychological Perspective*. New York: Cambridge University Press.

Kay, J. H. 1997. *Asphalt Nation: How the Automobile Took over America, and How We Can Take It Back*. Berkeley. University of California Press.

Landis, J. R., and G. G. Koch. 1977. "The Measurement of Observer Agreement for Categorical Data." *Biometrics* 33:159–74.

Lennard, S. H. C., and H. L. Lennard. 1987. *Livable Cities—People and Places: Social and Design Principles for the Future of the City*. Southampton, NY: Center for Urban Well-Being.

Llewelyn–Davies (consultants). 2000. *Urban Design Compendium*. London: English Partnerships/The Housing Corporation.

Lovasi, G. S., M. D. M. Bader, J. W. Quinn, K. M. Neckerman, C. Weiss, and A. Rundle. 2012. "Body Mass Index, Safety Hazards, and Neighborhood Attractiveness: An Examination of Independent Associations and Environment-Environment Interactions." *American Journal of Preventive Medicine* 43 (4): 378–84.

Lynch, K. 1960. *The Image of the City*. Cambridge, MA: Joint Center for Urban Studies.

———. 1962. *Site Planning*. Cambridge, MA: MIT Press.

Marshall, W. E., and N. W. Garrick. 2011. "Does Street Network Design Affect Traffic Safety?" *Accident Analysis and Prevention* 43 (3): 769–81.

McMillan, T. E. 2005. "Urban Form and a Child's Trip to School: The Current Literature and a Framework for Future Research." *Journal of Planning Literature* 19 (4): 440–56.

———. 2007. "The Relative Influence of Urban Form on a Child's Travel Mode to School." *Transportation Research A* 41 (1): 69–79.

Nasar, J. L. 1987. "The Effect of Sign Complexity and Coherence on the Perceived Quality of Retail Scenes." *Journal of the American Planning Association* 53:499–509.

Nasar, J. L., and A. E. Stamps. 2009. "Infill McMansions: Style and the Psychophysics of Size." *Journal of Environmental Psychology* 29 (1): 110–23.

Neckerman, K. M., G. S. Lovasi, S. Davies, M. Purciel, J. Quinn, E. Feder, N. Raghunath, B. Wasserman, and A. Rundle. 2009. "Disparities in Urban Neighborhood Conditions: Evidence from GIS Measures and Field Observation in New York City." *Journal of Public Health Policy* 30 (Supp. 1): S264–S285.

Nelessen, A. 1994. *Visions for a New American Dream*. Washington, DC: American Planning Association.

Odgers, C. L., A. Caspi, C. J. Bates, R. J. Sampson, and T. E. Moffitt. 2012. "Systematic Social Observation of Children's Neighborhoods Using Google Street View: A Reliable and Cost-Effective Method." *Journal of Child Psychology and Psychiatry* 53 (10): 1009–17.

Pikora, T., F. Bull, K. Jamrozik, M. Knuiman, B. Giles-Corti, and R. Donovan. 2002. "Developing a Reliable Audit Instrument to Measure the Physical Environment for Physical Activity." *American Journal of Preventive Medicine* 23 (3): 187–94.

Pikora, T., B. Giles-Corti, F. Bull, K. Jamrozik, and R. Donovan. 2003. "Developing a Framework for Assessment of the Environmental Determinants of Walking and Cycling." *Social Science and Medicine* 56:1693–703.

Placer County (CA). 2003. "Placer County Design Guidelines" (p. 115). http://www

.placer.ca.gov/Departments/CommunityDevelopment/Planning/Documents /~/media/cdr/Planning/documents/DesignGuides/DesignGuidelinesManual.ashx.

Pont, K., J. Ziviani, D. Wadley, S. Bennett, and R. Abbott. 2009. "Environmental Correlates of Children's Active Transportation: A Systematic Literature Review." *Health & Place* 15 (3): 827–40.

Purciel, M., and E. Marrone. 2006. "Observational Validation of Urban Design Measures for New York City: Field Manual." New York: Columbia University.

Purciel, M., K. M. Neckerman, G. S. Lovasi, J. W. Quinn, C. Weiss, M. D. M. Bader, R. Ewing, and A. Rundle. 2009. "Creating and Validating GIS Measures of Urban Design for Health Research." *Journal of Environmental Psychology* 29 (4): 457–66.

Rapoport, A. 1977. *Human Aspects of Urban Form: Towards a Man-Environment Approach to Urban Form and Design.* New York: Pergamon.

———. 1990. *History and Precedent in Environmental Design.* New York: Kluwer Academic Publishers, Plenum Press.

Raudenbush, S. W., and A. S. Bryk. 2002. *Hierarchical Linear Models: Applications and Data Analysis Methods.* 2nd ed. Thousand Oaks, CA: Sage.

Raudenbush, S. W., A. S. Bryk, and R. Congdon. 2004. *HLM 6 for Windows* (computer software). Skokie, IL: Scientific Software International, Inc.

Robert Wood Johnson Health & Society Scholars Program, Columbia University. 2006. "Aesthetic Features of Pedestrian-Friendly Cities." *Health & Society News* 2 (4): 1, 6. http://www.chssp.columbia.edu/newsletters/pdf/164_10.pdf.

Rundle, A. G., M. D. M. Bader, C. A. Richards, K. M. Neckerman, and J. O. Teitler. 2011. "Using Google Street View to Audit Neighborhood Environments." *American Journal of Preventive Medicine* 40 (1): 94–100.

Saelens, B. E., J. F. Sallis, and L. D. Frank. 2003. "Environmental Correlates of Walking and Cycling: Findings from the Transportation, Urban Design, and Planning Literatures." *Annals of Behavioral Medicine* 25 (2): 80–91.

Salingaros, N. A. 2000. "Complexity and Urban Coherence." *Journal of Urban Design* 5:291–316.

Sitte, C. 1889. *City Planning according to Artistic Principles.* Vienna: Verlag von Carl Graeser. (Complete translation in G.R. Collins, C.C. Collins, and Camillo Sitte, *The Birth of Modern City Planning* [New York: Rizzoli International, 1986].)

Stamps, A. E. 1998a. "Complexity of Architectural Silhouettes: From Vague Impressions to Definite Design Features." *Perceptual and Motor Skills* 87 (3, pt. 2): 1107–17.

———. 1998b. "Measures of Architectural Mass: From Vague Impressions to Definite Design Features." *Environment and Planning B* 25:825–36.

———. 1999. "Sex, Complexity, and Preferences for Residential Facades." *Perceptual and Motor Skills* 88:1301–12.

———. 2001. "Evaluating Enclosure in Urban Sites." *Landscape and Urban Planning* 57 (1): 25–42.

———. 2005. "Enclosure and Safety in Urbanscapes." *Environment and Behavior* 37 (1): 102–33.

Stamps, A. E., J. L. Nasar, and K. Hanyu. 2005. "Planner's Notebook: Using Pre-construction Validation to Regulate Urban Skylines." *Journal of the American Planning Association* 71:73–91.

Stamps, A. E., and S. Smith. 2002. "Environmental Enclosure in Urban Settings." *Environment and Behavior* 34 (6): 781–94.

Stead, D., and S. Marshall. 2001. "The Relationships between Urban Form and Travel Patterns: An International Review and Evaluation." *European Journal of Transport and Infrastructure Research* 1 (2): 113–41.

Trancik, R. 1986. *Finding Lost Space: Theories of Urban Design*. New York: Van Nostrand Reinhold.

Tunnard, C., and B. Pushkarev. 1963. *Man-Made America: Chaos or Control?* New Haven, CT: Yale University Press.

Unwin, R. 1909. *Town Planning in Practice*. London: T. Fisher Unwin. Reprint, New York: Princeton Architectural Press, 1994.

von Hoffman, A. 1996. "High Ambitions: The Past and Future of American Low-Income Housing Policy." *Housing Policy Debate* 7 (3): 423–46.

Whyte, W. H. 1980. *The Social Life of Small Urban Spaces*. Washington, DC: Conservation Foundation.

———. 1988. *City: Rediscovering the Center*. New York: Doubleday.

Wilson, J. S., C. M. Kelly, M. Schootman, E. A. Baker, A. Banerjee, M. Clennin, and D. K. Miller. 2012. "Assessing the Built Environment Using Omnidirectional Imagery." *American Journal of Preventive Medicine* 42 (2): 193–99.

Index